The **Adversary**

The

Adversary

A TRUE STORY OF
MONSTROUS DECEPTION

EMMANUEL CARRÈRE

Translated by Linda Coverdale

METROPOLITAN BOOKS

Henry Holt and Company | New York

Metropolitan Books
Henry Holt and Company, LLC
Publishers since 1866
115 West 18th Street
New York, New York 10011

Metropolitan Books™ is an imprint of
Henry Holt and Company, LLC.

Originally published in French as *L'Adversaire* by
P.O.L éditeur, Paris, in 2000.

Library of Congress Cataloging-in-Publication Data
Carrère, Emmanuel, 1957–
[Adversaire. English]
The adversary / Emmanuel Carrère ; translated by Linda Coverdale.
p. cm.
ISBN 0-8050-6583-0
1. Romand, Jean-Claude, 1954– 2. Murderers—France—Gex
Region—Biography. 3. Swindlers and swindling—France—Gex
Region. 4. Murders—France—Gex Region—Case
studies. I. Title.
HV6535.F8 G47313 2000
364.15'23'094477—dc21   00-040755

Henry Holt books are available for special promotions and
premiums. For details contact: Director, Special Markets.

First American Edition

Designed by Kelly S. Too

Printed in the United States of America
1 2 3 4 5 6 7 8 9 10

The **Adversary**

On the Saturday morning of January 9, 1993, while Jean-Claude Romand was killing his wife and children, I was with mine in a parent-teacher meeting at the school attended by Gabriel, our eldest son. He was five years old, the same age as Antoine Romand. Then we went to have lunch with my parents, as Jean-Claude Romand did with his, whom he killed after their meal. I usually devote Saturday afternoons and Sundays to my family, but I spent the rest of that weekend alone in my studio because I was finishing up a book I had been working on for over a year, a biography of the science fiction writer Philip K. Dick. The last chapter described the days he spent in a coma before his death. I completed it on Tuesday evening and on Wednesday morning opened my newspaper to the lead article on the Romand case.

Luc Ladmiral was awakened shortly after four o'clock Monday morning by a telephone call from Jacques Cottin, the pharmacist in Prévessin. The Romands' house was on fire; their friends should come try to salvage as much of the furniture as possible. When Luc arrived, the firemen were bringing out the bodies. All his life he will remember the sealed gray plastic bags into which they had put the children: too horrible to look at. Florence had simply been covered with a coat. Her face, blackened by the smoke, was unmarked. Smoothing her hair in a desolate gesture of farewell, Luc's fingers encountered something strange. He felt around, carefully tilting the young woman's head to one side, then called over a fireman to show him, at the base of the skull, an open wound. It must have been from a beam that fell on her, the fireman said; part of the attic had collapsed. Luc then clambered into the red truck where the rescuers had placed Jean-Claude, the only one of the family who was still alive. His pulse was weak. He was in pajamas, unconscious, burned yet already as cold as a corpse.

An ambulance arrived and took him away to the closest major hospital, across the border in Geneva. It was dark, chilly, and the jets of water from the fire hoses had drenched everyone. Since there was nothing more to be done at the scene, Luc went to the Cottins' house to dry off. In the yellow light of the kitchen, they listened to the sputtering of the coffee pot, not daring to look at one another. Their hands shook when they raised their cups, and as they stirred their coffee, the spoons made a dreadful racket. Then Luc went home to tell Cécile and the children what had happened. Sophie, their eldest, was Jean-Claude's goddaughter. A few days earlier, as she often did, she had slept over at the Romands' house, and she might very well have slept there again that night and wound up, like her playmates, in a gray plastic bag.

THEY HAD BEEN FRIENDS EVER SINCE MEDICAL SCHOOL IN Lyon. They'd gotten married almost at the same time; their children had grown up together. Each knew everything about the other's life—the public image, but also the secrets, the secrets of honest, reliable men who were all the more vulnerable to temptation. When Jean-Claude had confided in him about an affair, talked about chucking everything, Luc had made him listen to reason: "And you'll do the same for me, when it's my turn to be an ass." A friendship like that is one of the precious things in life, almost as precious as a successful marriage, and Luc had always been certain that one day, when they were sixty or seventy years old, they would look back together as from a mountaintop, after all that time, on the road they had traveled: the places where they'd stumbled, almost gotten lost; the ways they'd helped each other, and how, in the end, they'd come through everything. A friend, a true friend, is also a witness, someone whose attention affords you a clearer look at your own life, and for twenty years each of them had unfailingly, without any fuss, played this role for the other. Their lives were very similar, even if they hadn't succeeded in the same way. Jean-Claude had become a leading figure in the world of research, hobnobbing with government ministers, always off at international conferences, while Luc was a general practitioner in Ferney-Voltaire. But Luc wasn't jealous. The only thing that had come between them was an absurd disagreement, during the last few months, regarding their children's school. For some unfathomable reason, Jean-Claude had really gotten on his high horse, so Luc had had to take the first step, saying that they weren't going to quarrel over such a silly thing. The whole business had upset Luc; he and Cécile had talked it over several evenings in a row. How trivial it seemed now! How fragile life is! Only yesterday, there was a close, happy family, people who loved one another, and today—a boiler accident, charred bodies being taken to the morgue . . . His wife and children were everything to Jean-Claude. What would his life be like if he survived?

Luc phoned the emergency room in Geneva: the patient had been placed in a hyperbaric oxygen chamber; the prognosis was guarded.

Luc prayed with Cécile and the children that he would never regain consciousness.

WHEN LUC WENT TO OPEN HIS OFFICE, TWO POLICEMEN were waiting for him. Their questions seemed odd. They wanted to know if the Romands had any known enemies, if they'd been involved in any suspicious activities . . . Seeing Luc's astonishment, the police told him the truth. An initial examination of the bodies revealed that the victims had died *before* the fire, Florence from head injuries inflicted by a blunt instrument, Antoine and Caroline from bullet wounds.

That wasn't all. In Clairvaux-les-Lacs, in the Jura Mountains, Jean-Claude's uncle had been delegated to break the tragic news to the injured man's parents, a frail elderly couple. Accompanied by their doctor, he had gone to see them and found the house locked, the dog mysteriously silent. Worried, the uncle had broken open the door to discover his brother, his sister-in-law, and the dog lying in their own blood. Like Antoine and Caroline, they had been shot to death.

Murdered. The Romands had been murdered. The word echoed through Luc's brain, stunning him. "Was it a robbery?" he asked, as if that word might reduce the horror of the other one to something rational. The police didn't know yet, but two crimes striking members of the same family fifty miles apart were more likely to be an act of revenge or a settling of accounts. The officers asked again about possible enemies, and Luc, at a loss, shook his head. Enemies? The Romands? Everyone loved them. If they had been killed, it had to have been by people who didn't know them.

The police needed to find out exactly what Jean-Claude did for a living. A doctor, the neighbors said, but he didn't have an office. Luc explained that he was a researcher at the World Health Organization, in Geneva. One of the officers telephoned, asking to speak to someone who worked with Dr. Romand, perhaps his secretary or one of his colleagues. The receptionist did not know any Dr. Romand. When the caller insisted, she connected him to the personnel director, who consulted his files and confirmed that there was no Dr. Romand at WHO.

Then Luc understood and felt hugely relieved. Everything that had happened since four that morning—Cottin's phone call, the fire, Florence's wound, the gray bags, Jean-Claude lying severely burned in the hyperbaric chamber, and now this business about crimes—all of it had happened with perfect verisimilitude, an impression of reality that left no room for suspicion, but now, thank God, the scenario was going awry, revealing itself as what it was: a bad dream. He was going to wake up in his bed. He wondered if he would remember everything and if he would dare tell Jean-Claude about it. "I dreamed that your house was on fire, that your wife, your children, your parents were murdered, and that you—you were in a coma and no one at WHO knew anything about you." Could one say that to a friend, even to one's best friend? The idea occurred to Luc (it would haunt him later on) that in this dream, Jean-Claude served as a double, bringing out into the open Luc's own fears—of losing his loved ones but also of losing himself, of discovering that behind his social facade he was nothing.

IN THE COURSE OF THAT DAY, REALITY BECAME EVEN MORE nightmarish. Summoned to the police station in the afternoon, Luc learned within five minutes that a note in Jean-Claude's handwriting confessing to the crimes had been found in his car and that everything people thought they knew about his career and professional activities was a sham. It had taken only a few telephone calls and elementary inquiries to tear off the mask. The World Health Organization? No one there had ever heard of him. The national registry of physicians? He wasn't listed. The hospitals in Paris where he was said to be on the medical staff? He was not accredited there, nor was he a graduate of the medical school in Lyon where Luc himself, and several others, swore nevertheless to have been students with him. He had begun his studies, yes, but had stopped taking his exams at the end of the second year, and from then on, everything was false.

At first, Luc simply refused to believe this. When someone tells you that your best friend, your daughter's godfather, the most respectable man you know has killed his wife, his children, his parents, and that in addition he has been lying to you about everything for years, isn't it normal to go on believing in him, even in the face of overwhelming proof? What kind of friendship would let itself be so easily convinced of its error? Jean-Claude could not be a murderer. There had to be a piece missing from the puzzle. It would be found—and everything would take on a new meaning.

For the Ladmirals, those days were an unspeakable ordeal. The disciples of Jesus saw him arrested, tried, executed as though he were the lowest of criminals, and yet, even though Peter faltered, they continued to have faith in him. On the third day they learned that they had been right to remain steadfast. Cécile and Luc tried with all their strength to stand fast. But on the third day, and even before, they had to admit that their hope was in vain and that they would have to live with not only the loss of those who had died but also the grief of trust betrayed, of life completely corrupted by lies.

IF THEY COULD AT LEAST HAVE PROTECTED THEIR CHILdren! Simply told them—and that was awful enough—that

Antoine and Caroline had perished with their parents in a fire. But there was no use trying to hush it up. Within a few hours, the region had been invaded by reporters, photographers, TV crewmen. They pestered everyone, even the schoolchildren, who all knew by Tuesday that Antoine, Caroline, and their mommy had been killed by their daddy, who had then set their house on fire. Many of them began to have dreams that their homes were burning and that their daddies were doing what Antoine's and Caroline's father had done. At the Ladmirals', Luc and Cécile had dragged their three children's mattresses into the master bedroom because no one dared sleep alone anymore. Without yet knowing what it was they had to explain, Luc and Cécile would sit on the edge of the mattresses, soothing, caressing, trying at least to reassure. But they could tell that their words had lost their former magical power. Doubt had crept in, which nothing except time could dispel. Both they and their children had been robbed of childhood, for never again would the little ones nestle in their arms with the trust that is miraculous but normal, at their age, in normal families, and it was in thinking about this, about what had been irreparably destroyed, that Luc and Cécile began to cry.

THE FIRST EVENING, THEIR GROUP OF FRIENDS GATHERED at their house, and they came over every evening that week. They stayed until three or four in the morning trying to weather the blow together. They forgot to eat, they drank too much, many began smoking again. These late nights weren't funeral wakes—in fact they were the liveliest evenings the house had ever known: the shock was so great it stirred up a maelstrom of questions and uncertainties that short-circuited bereavement. Each of them went at least once a day to the police station, either summoned there or to check on the progress of the investigation, and they talked about it all night long, comparing information, constructing hypotheses.

The Gex region is a plain some twenty miles wide stretching from the foot of the Jura to the edge of Lake Geneva. Although situated in French territory, it is essentially a residential suburb of Geneva, an aggregate of well-to-do villages that have become home to a colony of international officials who work in Switzerland, are paid in Swiss francs, and for the most part are not subject to income tax. All enjoy more or less the same way of life. They live in former farmhouses that have been comfortably remodeled. The husband drives to his office in a Mercedes. His wife does her shopping and attends to her charity work in a Volvo. The children go to the Ecole Saint-Vincent, an expensive private school in the shadow of Voltaire's château. Jean-Claude and Florence were familiar and valued members of this community, where they had kept up their social position, and now everyone who knew them was wondering: Where had the money come from? If he wasn't who he claimed to be, what was he?

The prosecutor assigned to the case promptly announced to reporters that he was "prepared for anything"; then, after an initial examination of various bank accounts, he suggested that the motive behind the crimes was "the imposter's fear of being unmasked and the abrupt cessation of an as yet ill-defined illicit enterprise in which he was a key figure and which for years had been bringing in considerable amounts of money." This statement fired everyone's imagination. People started talking about trafficking in arms, currency, organs, narcotics . . . a vast criminal syndicate operating in the disintegrating former socialist bloc . . . the Russian mafia. Jean-Claude traveled a lot. The previous year, he had gone to Leningrad, bringing back some nesting dolls for Sophie, his goddaughter. In a fit of paranoia, Luc and Cécile wondered if these dolls concealed compromising documents, microfilm, or a microprocessor—something that the killers in Prévessin and Clairvaux might have searched for in vain. Because Luc, who was finding himself more and more isolated, still wanted to believe in some kind of plot. Perhaps Jean-Claude was a spy, a peddler of scientific or industrial secrets, but he couldn't have killed his family. *They* had killed them, *they* had concocted evidence to frame him for the crimes, *they* had even gone so far as to destroy the traces of his past.

"AN ORDINARY ACCIDENT, AN INJUSTICE CAN BRING ON madness. Forgive me Corinne, forgive me my friends, forgive me good people of the Saint-Vincent school board who wanted to punch my face in."

That was the text of the farewell note left in the car. What ordinary accident? What injustice? wondered the "friends," who all gathered at the Ladmirals' every evening. Several of them were also among the "good people," members of the school board, and the police went after them relentlessly. Each person had to provide a detailed account of the disagreement provoked at the beginning of the school year by the replacement of the principal. The police listened almost distrustfully. Wasn't that it, the injustice that had caused the tragedy? The members of the board were dismayed; they had argued, yes, perhaps someone had even talked about punching Jean-Claude in the nose—but you'd have to be crazy to imagine a connection between that quarrel and the massacre of an entire family! You would have to be crazy, the police admitted, and yet the connection had to exist.

Appalling evidence came from Corinne (the newspapers, which had been instructed not to give her name, called her a "mysterious mistress"). The previous Saturday, Jean-Claude had met her in Paris; they were to dine in Fontainebleau with his illustrious friend Bernard Kouchner, one of the founders of Doctors Without Borders. A few hours earlier, according to the autopsy, Jean-Claude had slain his wife, his children, and his parents. Of course, Corinne had had no idea of what he had done. En route to their dinner engagement, in a remote corner of the forest, he had tried to kill her as well. When she had resisted, he had backed off and then driven her home, saying that he was gravely ill and that this explained his attack of madness. Learning of the slaughter on Monday and realizing that she had almost become the sixth victim, Corinne had contacted the police, who had called Bernard Kouchner. He had never heard of Dr. Romand and had no house in Fontainebleau.

Everybody knew Corinne in Ferney, where she had lived before her divorce and subsequent move to Paris. No one, however, was aware that she had had an affair with Jean-Claude except for Luc and his wife, who held it against her. They considered Corinne a troublemaker, capable of saying anything at all to make herself interesting. But since the theory of some sort of plot became less tenable with each passing day, a crime of passion conveniently filled the gap. Luc recalled what Jean-Claude had confided to him and how deeply depressed his friend had been after the affair ended. Luc could easily imagine how Corinne might have driven Jean-Claude insane if they'd gotten back together: the shuttling between his wife and mistress, the growing tangle of lies, and on top of that the anguish of illness . . . Because Jean-Claude had also confessed to him that he was suffering from cancer, for which he was being treated in Paris by the eminent oncologist Léon Schwartzenberg. Luc mentioned this to the police, who checked his information. Dr. Schwartzenberg didn't know Jean-Claude any more than Kouchner did, and the inquiry, which was expanded to include the oncology departments of every hospital in France, never turned up any file anywhere for a Jean-Claude Romand.

THROUGH HER LAWYER, CORINNE SUCCEEDED IN FORCING the press to stop calling her the monster's mistress and to refer to her as just "a friend." Then it was learned that she'd handed over to him 900,000 francs in savings that he was to have invested for her in Switzerland and that he had embezzled instead. The mysterious smuggling intrigue turned out to be a common swindle. There was no more mention of espionage or organized crime. The investigators thought that he had betrayed the trust of others in his circle, and reporters hinted that these people didn't dare make a fuss because the investments he'd tempted them into were illegal: that explained, perhaps, why the prominent citizens of Ferney were acting so aloof . . . These insinuations exasperated Luc. As the murderer's "best friend," he was besieged by strangers in leather jackets who waved press cards, stuck microphones in his face, and offered him small fortunes to go through his photo albums. He systematically turned them away, to avoid tarnishing the memory of the dead, and the result was—he was suspected of tax fraud.

Other revelations came from Florence's family, the Crolets, who lived in Annecy and whom the Ladmirals knew well. They, too, had entrusted money to Jean-Claude: the father's retirement bonus plus, after his death, a million francs netted from the sale of his house. And not only did they know that this money, the fruit of a lifetime's labor, was irrevocably lost, but their grief was compounded by an agonizing suspicion: M. Crolet had died in a fall on a staircase when he was alone with Jean-Claude. Had he been yet another victim of his son-in-law?

EVERYONE WAS WONDERING: HOW COULD WE HAVE LIVED beside this man for so long without suspecting a thing? Everyone tried to remember a moment when some suspicion, something that might have led to some suspicion, had almost crossed their minds. The president of the school board kept telling people how he had not been able to find Jean-Claude in the directory of international agencies. Luc himself remembered that he'd been struck by something a few months earlier, after learning from Florence that Jean-Claude had ranked fifth on his medical board exam in Paris. What astonished Luc wasn't this achievement but the fact that he hadn't learned of it at the time. Why hadn't Jean-Claude mentioned it? Questioned, accused of being secretive, Jean-Claude had shrugged, said he didn't want to make a big deal of it, and changed the subject. It was extraordinary, this ability to deflect conversation whenever it turned to him. He did this so well that you didn't even realize it, and thinking back on it later, you wound up admiring his discretion, his modesty, his desire to show others to advantage instead of himself. Yet Luc had felt vaguely that there was something not quite right in what Jean-Claude said about his career. He'd considered calling WHO to discover exactly what it was he did there—but had decided the whole thing was absurd. And now he kept telling himself that if he'd gone through with it, maybe things would have turned out differently.

"Perhaps," said Cécile when he told her of his remorse, "—perhaps he would have killed you as well."

WHEN THEY SPOKE OF HIM, LATE AT NIGHT, THEY couldn't manage to call him Jean-Claude anymore. They didn't call him Romand, either. He was somewhere outside life, outside death, where he no longer had a name.

AFTER THREE DAYS, THEY LEARNED HE WAS GOING TO LIVE.

Made public on Thursday, the news hung heavily over his parents' funeral, which took place the next day in Clairvaux-les-Lacs. Services for Florence and the children had been put off to allow completion of the autopsies. These two circumstances made the ceremony even more unbearable. Standing there in the rain, how could one believe the words of peace and solace the priest forced himself to speak as the coffins were lowered into the ground? No one could find comfort in meditation, some calm inner space, some corner of decent grief where the soul could take refuge. Luc and Cécile were there, but since they barely knew the family, they stayed in the background. The flushed, rugged faces of these peasants of the Jura bore the stamp of sleepless nights, of helpless and obsessive brooding on death, denial, shame. Jean-Claude had been the pride of the village. They'd admired him for being so successful and yet remaining so simple, so close to his elderly parents. He had phoned them every day. Wishing to remain near them, he had refused a prestigious position in America, or so people said. In the two pages devoted to the story that day, a major Lyon news-paper published a photo taken in the sixth grade at the Clairvaux elementary school that showed Jean-Claude in the first row, smiling and sweet, with a caption that said: "Who would have believed that the model student would become a monster?"

The father had been shot in the back, the mother full in the chest. Certainly she—and perhaps both of them—had known that they were dying at the hands of their son, which meant that in the same instant they had seen death (which we all will see, which they had grown old enough to see in the fullness of their years) as well as the annihilation of everything that had given sense, happiness, and dignity to their lives. The priest promised that now they saw God. For believers, the moment of death is the moment when one sees God no longer through a glass darkly but face-to-face. Even nonbelievers believe in something of the sort, that in the instant of passing to the other side, the dying see the movie of their whole lives flash by, its meaning clear at last. And this vision that should have brought the elderly Romands the joy of accomplishment had been the triumph of deception and evil. They should have seen God and in his place they had seen, taking on the features of their beloved son, the one the Bible calls Satan, "the adversary."

You couldn't think of anything else: that stunned look, the bewilderment of betrayed children, in the old people's eyes; the half-charred little bodies of Antoine and Caroline lying next to their mother on tables in the morgue; and then the other body, soft and heavy, that of the murderer who had been so close to everyone, so familiar, and who was slowly beginning to stir again in a hospital bed a few miles away. He was suffering from burns, smoke inhalation, and the barbiturates he had taken, the doctors said, but they expected him to regain full consciousness over the weekend and to be well enough by Monday to be interrogated. Right after the fire, when everyone still thought it had been an accident, Luc and Cécile had prayed for him to die; that had been for his sake. Now they prayed for him to die, but it was for themselves, for their children, for all those who were still alive. That he himself should remain, death made man, in the world of the living, was a frightful threat hanging over them, the assurance that peace would never be restored, that the horror would never end.

. . .

ON SUNDAY, ONE OF LUC'S SIX BROTHERS ANNOUNCED that Sophie needed a new godfather. He offered to be her sponsor, asking her solemnly if she would accept him. With this family ceremony, the period of mourning began.

The previous autumn, Déa was dying of AIDS. She wasn't a close friend, but one of the best friends of one of our own best friends, Elisabeth. Déa was beautiful, with a somewhat unsettling loveliness now accentuated by her illness, and an unruly mane of which she was rather proud. Becoming quite pious toward the end, she set up at home a kind of altar with candles flickering before icons. One night, a candle set her hair on fire. She blazed up like a torch. She was taken to the burn unit of the Hôpital Saint-Louis. Third-degree burns over half her body: she would not die of AIDS, which is perhaps what she wanted. But she didn't die right away, lasting almost a week, during which Elisabeth went every day to see her—that is, to see what was left of her. She would stop by our place afterward to have a drink and talk. She said that in a certain way it's a beautiful place, a burn unit. There are white veils, gauze, silence; you'd think it was Sleeping Beauty's castle. All you could see of Déa was a figure wrapped in white bandages, and if she had been dead, the sight would have been almost peaceful. The dreadful thing was that she was still alive. According to her doctors, she was unaware of all this, and Elisabeth, who is a confirmed atheist, spent her nights praying for that to be true. As for me, I had reached the point in my biography of Philip Dick when he is writing that terrifying novel entitled *Ubik* and imagining what goes on in the brains of people who have been cryogenically preserved: drifting scraps of thought, clutter from ransacked stocks of memories, the stubborn nibbling of entropy, short circuits sparking gleams of panicked lucidity—and everything hidden by the steady, tranquil flow of an electroencephalogram that's *almost* flat. I was drinking and smoking too much and constantly felt as though I were going to wake up with a start. One night I couldn't stand it anymore. I got up, lay down again next to my sleeping wife, Anne, tossed and turned, every muscle tense, my nerves in tatters; I don't think I've ever in my life felt such mental and physical distress. Even the word *distress* isn't strong enough: I could feel rising in me, surging up, ready to overwhelm me, the nameless terror of someone buried alive. After several hours, quite suddenly, the tension subsided. I felt relaxed, at peace, and I realized I had broken into a flood of tears. Tears of joy. I had never felt such distress, and I had never felt such relief. For a moment I simply bathed uncomprehendingly in that almost amniotic ecstasy . . . and then I understood. I looked at the clock. The next day I telephoned Elisabeth. Yes, Déa had died. Yes, just before four in the morning.

STILL IN A COMA, HE ALONE WAS UNAWARE THAT HE WAS alive and that those he loved had died by his hand. This oblivion was not going to last. He would emerge from limbo. What would he see when he opened his eyes? A room painted white; white bandages enveloping his body. What would he remember? What images would come with him as he floated up toward the surface? Who would be the first one to meet his eyes? A nurse, probably. Was she going to smile at him, the way they all must do? Because at such moments, a nurse is a mother welcoming her child at the end of a very long tunnel, and they all know instinctively (or they would have chosen a different profession) that it is vital to be welcomed, as you leave this tunnel, by light, warmth, a smile. Yes, but, smile at *him*? The nurse had to know who he was; she was probably fending off reporters camped at the entrance to the ward, but reading their articles. She'd seen the pictures, always the same ones: the burned-out house and the six small identification photos. The sweet, timid old lady. Her husband, stern as justice, staring out from behind his heavy tortoiseshell glasses. Florence, smiling and lovely. Him, with the pleasant face of a contented father, slightly chubby, slightly balding. And then the two little ones, above all the two little ones, Antoine and Caroline, five and seven years old. I'm looking at their photos as I write this; Antoine somewhat resembles Jean-Baptiste, my youngest son. I imagine Antoine's laughter, his faint lisp, his tantrums, his seriousness, the things that were important to him, all that teddy-bear sentimentality which is the truth of the love we feel for our children—and now I feel like crying too.

HAVING DECIDED TO WRITE ABOUT THE ROMAND CASE, AS I quickly did, I considered rushing to the scene, setting up shop at a hotel in Ferney-Voltaire, playing the nosy, tenacious reporter. But I couldn't see myself sticking my foot in the doors the grieving families would want to slam in my face, spending hours drinking mulled wine with the local policemen, scheming how I could strike up an acquaintance with the examining magistrate's clerk. I realized that this wasn't what interested me. The investigation I might have made on my own, the judicial inquiry I might have tried to tap for secrets—these would bring only facts to light. The details of Romand's embezzlements, the way his double life had taken shape over the years, the roles various people had played, all that, which I would learn in good time, wouldn't tell me what I really wanted to know: what went on in his head during those days he supposedly spent in the office, days he didn't spend, as was first believed, trafficking in arms or industrial secrets, days he spent, it was now thought, walking in the woods? (I remember this sentence, the last one in a *Libération* article, which hooked me for good: "And he went off wandering, alone, in the forests of the Jura.")

No one—neither the judge, nor the witnesses, nor the psychiatric experts—could answer the question that was driving me to begin work on a book, except Romand himself. Since he was still alive, it was Romand or nobody. After six months of hesitation, I decided to write to him in care of his lawyer. It was the hardest letter I've ever written.

Paris, August 30, 1993

Monsieur,

My proposal may well offend you. I'll take a chance anyway.

I am a writer, the author to date of seven books; I enclose a copy of my latest work. Ever since reading about your case in the newspapers I have been haunted by the tragedy of which you were the agent and sole survivor. I would like to try to understand as much as possible of what happened and to make a book out of it—a book that could only be published, of course, after your trial.

Before I embark on this venture, it is important to me to learn how you feel about such a project. Interested, hostile, indifferent? You may be sure that in the second case, I would abandon my plan. In the first, on the other hand, I hope that you will consent to reply to my letters and perhaps, if it is allowed, to receive a visit from me.

I should like you to understand that I am not approaching you out of some unhealthy curiosity or a taste for the sensational. What you have done is not in my eyes the deed of a common criminal, or that of a madman, either, but the action of someone pushed to the limit by overwhelming forces, and it is these terrible forces I would like to show at work.

Whatever your reaction to this letter may be, I wish you a great deal of courage and assure you of my deepest compassion.

Emmanuel Carrère

I mailed the letter. A few moments afterward—too late—I realized with dismay what effect the title of the accompanying book might have on the recipient: *I Am Alive and You Are Dead.*

I waited.

I told myself that if by some extraordinary chance Romand agreed to talk to me (to "receive a visit from me," as I had formally phrased it), if his lawyer, the examining magistrate, or the prosecutor's office didn't raise any objections, I'd be sailing into uncharted waters. If, as was more likely, Romand did not reply, I'd write a novel "inspired" by the case, I'd change the names, places, circumstances, I'd invent to suit myself: it would be fiction.

Romand did not reply. I wrote again to his lawyer, who refused even to tell me whether he had forwarded my letter and my book to his client.

Appeal denied.

I began a novel about a man who kisses his wife and children every morning, pretending to leave for work, then goes off to walk aimlessly in the snowy woods. After a few dozen pages, I found myself stuck. I gave up. The following winter, a book just came to me, the book I'd been trying in vain to write for seven years without even realizing it. I wrote it very quickly, almost as if I were taking dictation, and I knew right away that it was by far the best thing I'd ever done. It was centered on the image of a murderous father who wanders, alone, in the snow, and I thought that what had intrigued me in Romand's story had, along with certain elements from other unfinished projects, found its place there, a fitting place, and that with this narrative I'd put an end to that kind of obsession. Now I could finally go on to something else. To what? I had no idea, but I didn't worry about it. I had written the book I'd been destined to write. I was beginning to feel alive.

Bourg-en-Bresse, 9/10/95

Monsieur,

It is neither hostility nor indifference to your proposals that explains such a long delay in my response to your letter of 8/30/93. My lawyer persuaded me not to write you while the preliminary investigation was in progress. As it has just ended, my thoughts are more in order and my mind more at liberty (after three psychiatric examinations and 250 hours of interrogation) to help you realize your project. I was strongly influenced by another fortuitous event: I have just read your latest book, *Class Trip*, which I much admired.

If you still wish to meet me in a common desire to understand this tragedy that remains ever present to me, you will need to send a request for a visitation permit to the prosecutor, accompanied by two photos and a copy of your identification card.

I am looking forward to hearing from you or meeting you and I wish you every success with your book. Please be assured of my profound gratitude for your compassion and my admiration for your talent as a writer.

See you soon, perhaps.

Jean-Claude Romand

To say that I was shaken by this letter is an understatement. I felt as though someone had caught up with me after two years and were tugging at my sleeve. I had changed, and I thought I had left all that far behind. Now the case and especially my interest in it rather disgusted me. On the other hand, I wasn't going to tell him no, that I no longer wanted to meet him. I applied for a visitation permit. My request was denied since I was not a family member, although I was informed that I might renew my application after the prisoner's appearance before the criminal court, scheduled for the spring of 1996. In the meantime, there was still the mail.

ON THE BACKS OF HIS ENVELOPES HE PUT LITTLE STICKERS with his name and address, "M. Jean-Claude Romand, 6, rue du Palais, 01011 Bourg-en-Bresse," and when I wrote to him I avoided using the word *prison* on the envelope. I had the feeling that he wasn't happy with his prison-issue writing paper, the need to use it sparingly, perhaps even the requirement to write by hand. I stopped typing my letters so that in this respect, at least, we would be equals. My obsession with the inequality of our positions, my fear of wounding him by reveling in my good fortune as a free man, a respected writer, a happy husband and father, and my guilt over not being guilty—all this gave my first letters an almost obsequious tone that he faithfully echoed in his replies. I dare say there aren't thirty-six million ways of speaking to someone who has killed his wife, his children, his parents, and lives on after them. But I realize with hindsight that I immediately rubbed him the right way by adopting that note of pathetic and sympathetic gravity and by seeing him not as someone who had done something horrific but as someone to whom something horrific had happened, the unfortunate toy of diabolic forces.

I asked myself so many questions that I didn't dare ask him a single one. He, for his part, was as little inclined to go over past events as he was passionately keen on scrutinizing their meaning. He mentioned no memories, made only distant and abstract allusions to "the tragedy," none to those who had been its victims, but willingly went on at length about his own suffering, his impossible grief, and the psychoanalytic writings of Lacan, which he had begun reading in the hope of better understanding himself. He copied out for me excerpts of the psychiatrists' reports: "In this particular case, and at a certain archaic level of functioning,

J.C.R. was no longer able to distinguish very well between himself and his love objects: he was part of them and they of him in a cosmogonic system that was all-embracing, undifferentiated, and closed. At that level, there is no longer much difference between suicide and homicide."

Asking him for details about his life in prison didn't produce anything more concrete either. He seemed interested not in reality, only in the meaning hidden behind it, and ready to interpret everything that happened to him—particularly my intervention in his life—as a sign. He said he was convinced "that a writer's approach to this tragedy can largely complete and transcend other, more reductive visions, such as those of psychiatry or other human sciences" and he wished to persuade me as well as himself that "all 'narcissistic recuperation' " was "far from his mind (the conscious mind, at least)." I gathered that he was counting on me more than on the psychiatrists to explain his own story to him—and on me more than on the lawyers to explain it to the world. This responsibility frightened me, but after all, he hadn't come looking for me, I'd made the first move, and I felt I should accept the consequences.

I GAVE OUR CORRESPONDENCE A FRESH TWIST BY ASKING: "Are you a believer? What I mean is: Do you believe in a higher power that understands and may perhaps be able to forgive what you yourself fail to comprehend in this tragedy?"

Reply: "Yes. 'I believe I believe.' And I don't think it's a convenient belief designed to give a meaning to my life (and survival) in some mystical redemption or to deny the terrifying possibility that we will not all meet again after death in Eternal Love. Many 'signs' have appeared in the last three years to reinforce my conviction, but please understand my discretion on this subject. I do not know whether you yourself are a believer. Your first name might be a positive indication."

There again, I had started it. As awkward as the question was, I had to answer it with a yes or no, and groping in the dark, I said yes. "Otherwise, I could not confront a story as harrowing as yours. To face, without morbid complacency, the night into which you were plunged and where you still remain, one must believe there exists a light in which every-thing that has been, even the extremes of calamity and evil, will become clear to us."

AS THE TRIAL APPROACHED, HE BECAME MORE AND MORE anxious. What was at stake for him was not his punish-ment: the sentence would necessarily be a heavy one, he knew that, and I did not have the impression that he missed his freedom. Certain constraints weighed on him in prison, but on the whole the life suited him. Everyone knew what he had done, he didn't have to lie anymore, and aside from his suffering, he was enjoying a psychological liberty that was entirely new. He was a model prisoner, as respected by his companions as he was by the personnel. Leaving this cocoon in which he felt at home, being thrown on the mercy of people who considered him a fiend—that scared him. He kept telling himself that it had to be done, that it was essential for others and for himself that he not escape justice. "I'm preparing for this trial," he wrote me, "as if it were a crucial appointment: it will be the last with 'them,' the last chance to finally be myself before 'them.' . . . I have the feeling that I won't have much of a future after that."

I WANTED TO SEE THE PLACES WHERE HE HAD LIVED AS A phantom. I set out one week, provided with maps he had carefully drawn at my request, annotated itineraries that I followed faithfully, respecting even the chronological order he suggested to me. ("Thank you for giving me the chance to revisit this familiar world, a very painful trip but one easier to share with someone else than to undertake alone . . .") I saw the hamlet of his childhood, his parents' house, his student apartment in Lyon, the burned-down house in Prévessin, the Pharmacie Cottin where his wife had filled in behind the counter, the Ecole Saint-Vincent in Ferney. I had the name and address of Luc Ladmiral; I passed his office but did not go in. I spoke to no one. Alone, I dragged myself around where he'd dragged out his empty days, alone: on the forest trails of the Jura and, in Geneva, in the neighborhood of international organizations where

WHO has its headquarters. I'd read that a large photograph of this building was framed on the wall of the room where he killed his mother. An X on the facade marked his office window, but I didn't know where that X was and I didn't venture beyond the lobby.

I felt pity, a painful sympathy, following in the footsteps of that man wandering aimlessly, year after year, harboring his absurd secret that he could confide to no one and that no one should learn on pain of death. Then I thought about the children, about the photos of their bodies taken at the morgue: raw horror that makes you instinctively shut your eyes, shake your head to erase it all from reality. I had thought I was finished with these tales of madness, confinement, freezing cold. I hadn't planned on warbling like Saint Francis about the dazzling beauty of the world and the nightingale's song, but still—I had thought I was free of that other stuff. And here I was again, chosen (a strong term, I know, but I don't see how I can say it any other way) by that atrocious story, drawn within the orbit of the man who had done *that*. I was afraid. Afraid and ashamed. Ashamed in front of my children, that their father should be writing about that. Was there still time to escape, or was it my particular vocation to try to understand that, to look it squarely in the face?

TO MAKE SURE OF A GOOD SEAT IN THE COURTROOM, I'D gotten myself a press pass from the weekly *Le Nouvel Obser-*

vateur. On the eve of the opening session, all of France's crime reporters descended on the largest hotel in Bourg-en-Bresse. Until then I'd been acquainted with only one kind of journalist, movie critics. Now I was discovering another, whose tribal gatherings are not festivals but trials. When they recall their campaigns—after some elbow-bending, which we did that evening—they speak not of Cannes, Venice, or Berlin but of Dijon and the trial of Villemin, the mother who drowned her child, or of Lyon and the Gestapo officer Klaus Barbie, and I found that much more serious. My first article on the proceedings won me some respect. An old hand from the daily *L'Est Républicain* chatted familiarly with me as he kept filling my glass, and the pretty girl from the Communist paper *L'Humanité* smiled at me. I felt I'd earned my wings from these people whose friendliness made me feel at home.

The defendant is the one who says yes or no to the presence of photographers when the trial begins, and Romand had said yes, which some people had seen as a sign of grandstanding. There were a good thirty photographers the next day and cameramen from every television network, who killed time by filming the empty witness box, the courtroom moldings, and, in front of the judge's bench, the glass case displaying the evidence: rifle, silencer, tear gas canister, photos from a family album. The children laughing as they splashed each other in an inflatable backyard pool. Antoine blowing out the candles on his fourth birthday. Florence looking on with tender confidence and pride. The accused didn't seem sad, either, in a picture that must have dated from his engagement to Florence or early in their marriage: they were at a table in a restaurant or at a banquet, people around them were having fun, he had his arm about her shoulders, and they seemed very much in love. He had a baby face, curly hair, a pleasant, dreamy expression. I wondered if he'd already begun lying when that picture was taken. No doubt he had.

The man the court officers led to the stand had the waxy complexion of a prisoner, close-cropped hair, a thin, flabby body melted down on what was still a heavy frame. He wore a black suit, a polo shirt open at the neck, and he confirmed his identity in a toneless voice. He kept his downcast eyes fixed on his clasped hands, from which the cuffs had just been removed. The reporters in front of him, the judge and jury to his right, the public on his left—all studied him, fascinated. "It's not every day you get to see the face of the Devil": that was how the next day's article in *Le Monde* began. In mine, I wrote: "of a man damned to hell."

Only Florence's family did not look at him. Sitting just in front of me, between her two sons, Florence's mother stared at the floor as if she were clinging to an invisible ledge to keep from falling into a faint. She had had to get out of bed that morning, choose clothes to wear, eat some breakfast, come from Annecy by car, and now she was here listening to the reading of the twenty-four-page indictment.

When the court clerk came to the autopsies performed on her daughter and grandchildren, the fist clenching a balled-up handkerchief pressed to her lips began to tremble slightly. I could have reached out and touched her shoulder, but there was an abyss between us that was more than the unbearable depth of her agony. It was not to her and her family that I had written but to the one who had destroyed their lives. It was to him that I felt I owed consideration because, wishing to tell this story, I saw it as *his* story. It was with *his* lawyer that I had lunch. I was on the other side.

He remained slumped, silent, still. Only toward the end of the morning did he risk looking over at the courtroom audience and the press section. His eyeglass frames glinted behind the window that separated him from all of us. When his eyes finally met mine, we both quickly looked away.

The Romands are a family of foresters in the Jura Mountains who have lived in the small town of Clairvaux-les-Lacs or the neighboring villages for several generations. There they form a veritable clan, respected for their austere and stubborn character: "That's a real Romand face," people say. Romands work hard, fear God, and their word is their bond.

Aimé Romand, born just after World War I, was drafted in 1939 and immediately taken prisoner, spending five years in a stalag. Home again, a decorated veteran, he worked with his father and eventually took over for him as the manager of a timber company. Since it is relatively easy to cheat when cutting trees, a timber manager must be completely trustworthy. Aimé, like his father, deserved such trust. Tall and bony, with piercing eyes, he inspired confidence even though he lacked the more cheerful charisma of his younger brother Claude, who owned a garage. Aimé married an unassuming little woman whom people came to think of as sickly without knowing exactly what was wrong with her. She had a delicate constitution and was constantly fretting. Perhaps because of her masked depression or a certain obsessiveness in Aimé, one senses in the couple something tense, overcritical, a long-standing habit of propriety and secretiveness. Romand families are the kind that swarm with children, but Aimé and his wife had only Jean-Claude, in 1954. Anne-Marie was later hospitalized twice for extra-uterine pregnancies that became life-threatening. The father tried to hide what was happening from his son so as not to frighten him and because what was happening belonged to the dirty and dangerous world of sex. The hysterectomy was camouflaged as appendicitis, but both times his mother went away the little boy deduced from her absence, from the sinister whispering of the word *hospital*, that she was dead and that her death was being concealed from him.

HIS EARLY CHILDHOOD WAS SPENT IN THE SMALL VILLAGE where his father ran a farm to which he devoted every moment not spent at his job with the timber company. I visited the hamlet, guided by Jean-Claude's maps: it's a tiny cluster of houses at the end of a narrow valley lost in a vast and gloomy forest of firs. The school had only three students.

Then his parents built a house in Clairvaux, and the family moved there. Jean-Claude was a year ahead of his age group and a great reader. In fifth grade, he was first in his class. Neighbors, cousins, schoolteachers all remember a well-behaved little boy, quiet and sweet, whom some are tempted to describe as too well-behaved, too quiet, too sweet, even while admitting that this excessiveness became clear to them after the fact, a feeble explanation for an inexplicable tragedy. An only child, perhaps somewhat overprotected by his mother. A child who never got up to any mischief, more respectable—if one can say that about a child—than truly lovable, but even so a child whom no one imagined to be unhappy. He himself rarely speaks of his father without slipping in a bizarre little flourish to the effect that the man deserved his first name, which means "beloved": "Aimé, the well-named," Jean-Claude calls him. He says that his mother worried all the time and that he learned early on to mislead her so that she wouldn't worry even more. He admired his father for never showing his feelings and tried to imitate him. Everything always had to be fine or else his mother would get worse, and it would have been heartless of him to make her feel worse over trifles, a child's little troubles. It was better to conceal them. In the village, for example, where he had many relatives, the households were livelier, but he sensed the pain his parents felt when he asked why he had no brother or sister. He felt that this question touched on something hidden and that his curiosity—but even more, his sadness—brought them sorrow. That was a word his mother used, *sorrow*, giving it a strangely concrete meaning, as if it were a physical disease eating away at her. He knew that by admitting that he, too, was suffering from this malady he would make his mother's illness worse, and hers was much more serious and might even prove fatal. On the one hand, he had been taught not to lie, and that was absolute dogma: a Romand was as good as his word, a Romand told the truth and shamed the Devil. On the other hand, there were certain things you shouldn't say, even if they were true. You had to avoid upsetting anyone, or boasting about your success or your good qualities.

(Wishing to give an example of this, he suddenly started talking about how he and his wife sometimes pretended to go to the movies in Geneva when they were actually teaching underprivileged families to read and write. They had never spoken of this to their friends, nor had he mentioned it to the examining magistrate, and when the puzzled judge tried to learn more from him—who were these families, what program was sponsoring this activity—he took refuge in the discretion he owed to Florence's memory: she wouldn't have wanted him to make a show of their generosity.)

WE WERE ABOUT TO MOVE ON FROM THE DEFENDANT'S childhood when Maître Abad, his lawyer, asked him, "So, when you had troubles or joys, didn't you turn to your dog as your pal?" Jean-Claude opened his mouth. We anticipated a banal reply, given in that reasonable and at the same time plaintive tone we had come to expect—but nothing came out. He swayed on the stand. He began to shiver slightly, then violently, throughout his body, and a kind of distraught humming issued from his mouth. Even Florence's mother turned to look at him. Then he flung himself to the ground, uttering a groan that made my blood run cold. We heard his head strike the floor, saw his legs flailing above the witness box. The policemen around him did their best to immobilize his tall frame, shaken by convulsions, and then led him out, still trembling and moaning.

I just wrote "made my blood run cold." I understood that day the truth of other set expressions: it really was "a deathly silence" that fell after he left, until the presiding judge, in a quavering voice, adjourned the proceedings for one hour. People didn't start talking, trying to make sense of what had happened, until they were outside the courtroom. The defendant had seemed so detached until then that some observers saw his fit as a welcome sign of emotion. Others found it monstrous that a man who had killed his children should have finally shown this emotion over a dog. Some wondered if he was faking. In theory, I had stopped smoking, but I bummed a cigarette from a newspaper sketch artist with a white beard and ponytail. "You've figured out what his lawyer's up to, haven't you?" he asked me. I hadn't figured it out. "He wants to make him crack. He knows that he needs some gut emotions here, that the public thinks his client's a cold fish, so he wants them to see his vulnerable side. But he doesn't realize—it's horribly dangerous to do that. I can tell you, I've been lugging my sketch pad around all the courtrooms of France for forty years, I've got a good eye. This guy is *very* sick, the psychiatrists are nuts to have let him go to trial. He's controlling himself, he controls everything, that's how he keeps hanging on, but if somebody starts poking him someplace where he can't maintain control anymore, he's going to come apart in front of everyone and, believe me, it's going to be god-awful. They think it's a man we've got in front of us, but in fact it's not a man anymore, hasn't been a man for a long, long time. It's like a black hole, you'll see, it's going to spring at our faces. People don't know what true madness is. It's dreadful. It's the most dreadful thing in the world."

I nodded. I was thinking of *Class Trip*, which Jean-Claude had told me was an accurate account of his childhood. I was thinking of the big white void that had slowly taken over inside him until all that was left was that semblance of a man dressed in black, that abyss whose chill was sending a shiver down the old artist's spine.

Court reconvened. Back on his feet after an injection, Jean-Claude tried to explain what had come over him. "Mentioning that dog—it reminded me of my childhood secrets, secrets that were hard to bear . . . Perhaps it's indecent to talk about my unhappiness as a child . . . I couldn't talk about it because my parents wouldn't have understood, would have been disappointed . . . I hadn't started lying then, but I never revealed my deepest feelings, except to my dog . . . I was always smiling, and I believe my parents never suspected my sadness . . . *I didn't have anything else to hide back then, but I hid that, this anguish, this sadness . . .* I'm sure they would have been willing to listen to me, Florence would have been willing, too, but I wasn't able to speak . . . and when you get caught in that endless effort not to disappoint people, the first lie leads to another, and then it's your whole life."

ONE DAY THE DOG DISAPPEARED. THE CHILD—AT LEAST according to the adult—suspected his father of shooting it with a rifle. Either because the dog was sick and the father wanted to spare his son the torment of watching it die or because the animal had done something so serious that execution was the only possible punishment. A last hypothesis would be that the father had told the truth, that the dog really did disappear, but it doesn't seem that the child ever considered this, so ingrained was the habit of the white lie in this family where the rule was never to tell a falsehood.

Throughout the trial, the dogs in his life evoked intense emotions in him. Not one of them, strangely enough, was mentioned by name. He came back to them time and again, dating events with reference to their illnesses and the worry these ailments caused him. Several people had the impression that he wanted, consciously or not, to express something by using the tears these stories brought to his eyes; they felt that something was trying to emerge through this breach and that this something, in the end, did not manage to come out.

AS A BOARDER AT THE LYCÉE IN LONS-LE-SAUNIER, HE WAS a solitary adolescent, bad at sports, intimidated not so much by girls—who lived on another planet—as by the savvier boys who claimed to hang out with them. He says he sought comfort in the company of an imaginary girlfriend named Claude; the psychiatrists wondered if he didn't invent her after the fact to humor them. There is no doubt, however, that he received the equivalent of an A- on his first baccalaureate examination and that from the three philosophy topics offered in his school district at the exam sitting of June 1971 he chose "Does truth exist?"

TO PREPARE FOR THE FORESTRY COMMISSION'S COMPETI-tive examination, he entered the prep class for the Institut National Agronomique at the prestigious Lycée du Parc, in Lyon, and there things didn't go too well. He talks about a bullying incident, while admitting that it wasn't anything malicious. Was he humiliated? He reacted by developing a series of sinus infections that allowed him to avoid returning to Lyon after the All Saints' holidays and to spend the rest of the school year holed up in his parents' house.

He is the only one who can say what that year in Clair-vaux was like, and he isn't telling. It's a blank in his life. Nights and the winter are long in a village in the Jura. One stays snug indoors, turning on the lights early, keeping an eye on the main street through gauze curtains and the fog. Men go to the café, but he never did. He rarely went out, spoke to no one except his parents, whom he had to keep convinced that he was physically ill because any form of melancholy or misgiving would have struck them as mere caprice. He was tall, bulky, with a flabby body, a frightened child already as big as an adult. His bedroom, which he hadn't really lived in during his years at boarding school, remained a child's room. It was to stay that way until the day, twenty-two years later, when he killed his father there. I imagine him stretched out on a bed that has grown too short for him, staring at the ceiling; suddenly and silently panicking because it's already dark outside; reading himself into a stupor. His parents didn't have many books besides some practical texts on forestry and housekeeping, a shelf devoted to World War II, and a few religious works. They mistrusted novels: only because their son was ill did they give him the money to buy some at the local newsstand, where the revolving rack of paperbacks wasn't often restocked with fresh titles. They had registered him in a correspondence course. Every week—it was something of an event at the house, where they didn't receive much mail—

the postman would bring a fat salmon-colored envelope, its flap poorly sealed, containing the exercises to be completed and sent back in the same envelope, which would eventually return with the corrected and graded homework, as well as new assignments. He went along with the ritual, but did he really learn the lessons? In any case, there must have been a period when he followed the program simply for appearance's sake and, without daring to announce it, decided not to return to the prep class for the Institut National Agronomique, thus abandoning plans for a career in the Forestry Commission.

THEY WANTED HIM TO BECOME A FORESTER; HE CHOOSES to study medicine. This change in direction seems at first glance to show that he had the backbone to stand up for his own wishes in the face of opposition. Yet he says he made this decision with regret. All through his dossier, he speaks at length about his love of the woods, a love inherited from Aimé, who considered each tree a living creature and thought long and hard before selecting one to be cut down. Since the life of a tree can span six human generations, that was the yardstick he used to measure the life of a man, organically connected to three generations of forebears and three of descendants. Jean-Claude says he couldn't imagine anything more beautiful than to live and work in the forest as his family had always done. Why did he abandon that way of life? I think he did in fact dream of becoming a forester like his father, because he saw that his father was respected, invested with real authority; in short, he admired him. Then, at the Lycée du Parc, his admiration ran up against the disdain of the well-dressed, middle-class sons of doctors or lawyers, boys who saw a forestry manager as some kind of minor official with muddy boots. His father's profession, even at a higher level, with a university degree, no longer seemed desirable to him, and he must have felt ashamed of this. To move up the social ladder, he devised a plan that was quite reasonable, given his good grades, a plan he could achieve by becoming a doctor, and he felt torn— like any sensitive person who rises above his station—by this betrayal of his family even as he was fulfilling their fondest hopes. "I knew what a disappointment it would be for my father," he says, but his father doesn't seem to have been disappointed in the slightest. A bit worried in the beginning, he was soon naively proud of his son's success. So Jean-Claude must admit that the bitter disappointment was *his* and that he chose medicine as a last resort, something for which he felt not the least inclination.

To him, the idea of caring for patients and touching ailing bodies was repulsive, and he never made any secret of this. The prospect of learning about diseases intrigued him, however. One of the psychiatrists who examined him, Dr. Toutenu, said at the trial that he disagreed with the defendant's claim to have had no medical vocation. It is Dr. Toutenu's belief that Jean-Claude had the potential to become a real doctor, a fine one, and that in choosing his career he was impelled by one of those powerful unconscious motives without which nothing is accomplished: the desire to understand his mother's illness, perhaps even to cure it. And as it was difficult in this family to discriminate between forbidden psychological suffering and its approved organic manifestations, Dr. Toutenu ventured so far as to say that Jean-Claude would have made an excellent psychiatrist.

THERE WAS ANOTHER REASON TO REGISTER AS A FIRST-year med student in Lyon: a distant cousin, whom he sometimes saw at family gatherings, would be going to medical school there as well. Florence lived in Annecy with her parents and her two younger brothers. Her father worked in a firm that manufactured eyeglass frames; one of her brothers was an optician. She was a tall, athletic girl with a good figure who loved campfires, going out with friends, baking cakes for church fairs. She was an observant Catholic without being self-conscious about it. Everyone who knew her describes her as frank, honest, plainspoken, happy to be alive. "A really nice girl," says Luc Ladmiral, "a bit old-fashioned." Not stupid at all but not cunning, either, in the sense that she was as naive about evil as she was incapable of doing it. She seemed destined for an uneventful life, one whose course would have seemed dispiriting to the cynical souls whom she did not care to know: university studies, not too advanced, pursued long enough for her to find a husband as down-to-earth and warmhearted as she was; two or three lovely children raised with firm principles and high spirits; a house in the suburbs with a well-equipped kitchen; big parties for Christmas and birthdays, young and old mixing happily together; friends of her own sort; a lifestyle that would improve at a modest but steady rate; then the departure of the children, one by one, their marriages, the oldest son's bedroom made over into a music room because now there's time to take up the piano again; the husband retires, time seems to have just flown by, she begins having attacks of the blues, finding the house too big, the days too long, the children's visits too few and far between; she finds herself thinking about that guy with whom she had a brief affair, the only one, early in her forties, such a wrenching experience—the secrecy, the giddiness, the guilt, later on the discovery that the husband had his fling as well, that he'd even thought about divorce; she shivers at the approach of autumn, All Saints' Day is here already and one morning, after a routine exam, she learns she's got cancer and that's it, it's over, in a few months she'll be dead and buried. An ordinary life, but she would have been able to carry it off, to inhabit it the way a good housewife knows how to cherish the soul of a home and make it pleasant for her family. She doesn't seem to have ever longed for anything different. Perhaps she was protected by her faith, which people say was profound. She never displayed the slightest tendency toward romantic fantasy, did not seem at all cut out for flings, frivolity, or, of course, tragedy.

(Having said that, I should add that before the tragedy occurred, everyone thought Jean-Claude was the perfect husband for such a woman. During the trial, the judge was shocked by his purchases of adult videos and ingenuously asked him what he did with them. When the defendant said that he watched them, sometimes in the company of his wife, the judge accused him of slandering the memory of the deceased. "Can anyone imagine Florence watching pornographic videos?" she exclaimed, and he, bowing his head, murmured in reply, "No, I understand that, but no one imagined me doing it, either.")

THIS STRAIGHT, BRIGHT PATH THROUGH LIFE THAT SEEMED a natural part of Florence was something he wanted to share. He says that from the age of fourteen on he'd considered himself engaged to her. Nothing stood in their way, but it isn't clear that the choice was a mutual one right from the beginning. Florence shared a small apartment in Lyon with two girls who were also medical students. If they are to be believed, Florence was irritated by the timid yet insistent courtship of this cousin from the Jura who appealed more to her parents and who, instructed by them to watch over her, never failed to wait for her at the train station when she returned from Annecy every Sunday night. She was quite sociable, whereas he knew no one, but by tagging along he eventually worked his way into her circle of friends. No one had any objection to him, and if he wasn't there no one ever thought about calling him up, either. In this boisterous but well-behaved little group, whose members enjoyed hiking in the mountains and sometimes went out to clubs on Saturday nights, Jean-Claude played the role of the bookworm, someone not particularly amusing but pleasant enough. It was Luc Ladmiral who was the natural leader. Handsome, from a well-established family of Lyonese doctors, sure of himself yet unpretentious, Catholic without being narrowminded, concerned about his future but determined to enjoy his youth, he got along perfectly with Florence, and they were the best of pals. Jean-Claude used to lend him his class notes, so neatly written they seemed intended to be read by others. Luc valued Jean-Claude's reliability and loyalty. Whenever he praised him, he liked to emphasize the soundness of his own judgment, which wasn't taken in by appearances: where others saw only a placid, slightly dull country bumpkin, Luc detected a hard worker who would go far and, even better, a man worthy of trust, without guile, in whom one could have complete confidence. Their friendship did much to smooth Jean-Claude's way into the group and may have had some influence on Florence's feelings.

Gossip has it that she gave in to Jean-Claude simply because he wore her down, that she was touched by his devotion, perhaps fond of him, but not in love with him. Who knows? Who can say what mysteriously brings two people together? What we do know is that for seventeen years they celebrated the first of May, which wasn't their anniversary but the day when Jean-Claude had dared to say "I love you" to Florence, and that after this declaration he experienced with her (and she, quite probably, with him) an initiation into sexual relations. He was twenty-one years old.

SEX IS ONE OF THE BLANKS IN THIS STORY. BY HIS OWN admission, until Corinne he had never known any woman except his wife, and although I may be mistaken, I don't think Florence had any adventures after her marriage. The number of partners has no bearing on the quality of a love life, and many happy erotic relationships must exist between people who remain faithful to each other throughout their lives—yet it's hard to imagine that Jean-Claude and Florence Romand were united by a joyous erotic bond, for if they had been their story would have turned out differently. When the question was put to him during the preliminary investigation, he merely replied that everything was "normal" and, rather curiously, not one of the psychiatrists who examined him tried to draw him out on the subject or formulate any hypotheses of their own. During the trial, however, a few veteran reporters mockingly suggested that at the bottom of the whole mess was the defendant's inadequacy in bed. This rumor was based not only on the general impression he created but also on a coincidence: each time he first slept with a woman (Florence in the spring of 1975,

Corinne in the spring of 1990), the union was followed by a separation imposed by his partner and a period of depression for him. As soon as Corinne gave in to his advances, she made him an affectionate and reasonable little speech to the effect of, Let's stop now, our friendship is too important to me to risk spoiling it, believe me, it's better this way, etc. A speech he listened to as though he were a chastised child someone was trying to console by telling him it was for his own good. Likewise, fifteen years earlier, after a few days of what was finally a sexual relationship, Florence used the pretext of needing to concentrate on her exams to decide that they'd better not see each other anymore. Yes, that would be best.

Given the brush-off, he reacted as he had at the Lycée du Parc, with hidden depression and a subconsciously deliberate mistake. Whether his alarm clock didn't ring or he didn't want to hear it, he got up too late to take one of his final exams at the end of his second year. This wasn't a catastrophe, as he was able to reschedule the exam for September and needed only a few more points to pass. The summer was nevertheless a sad one, because although Florence still refused to see him—for the good of both his and her studies—he knew through mutual friends that her determination did not keep her from going out with pals and having a good time while he was moping off in Clairvaux. Then classes began again, and his life started to split in two.

.   .   .

BETWEEN HIS SEPARATION FROM FLORENCE AND THE
beginning of classes in September, a telling episode
occurred. They were in a nightclub, the usual gang minus
Florence, who had already left for Annecy. At one point,
Jean-Claude said he was going out to get some cigarettes
from his car. He didn't return until several hours later,
apparently without anyone's noticing his long absence. His
shirt was torn and stained with blood, and he seemed distraught. He told Luc and the others that strangers had
attacked him for no reason. Threatening him with a gun,
they had taken his keys, forced him into the trunk of his
car, then driven off. The car had sped along, jolting him
around in the trunk, bruised and terrified. He'd had the
impression they were driving a long way and that these guys
he'd never seen before, who had perhaps mistaken him for
someone else, were going to kill him. As brutally and unac-
countably as they'd thrown him into the trunk, they finally
hauled him out of it, beating him up and abandoning him
by the side of the road to Bourg-en-Bresse, thirty miles outside of Lyon. They'd left him his car, in which he'd driven
back as best he could.

"But what did they want with you?" exclaimed his
friends in amazement. He shook his head: "That's just it, I
haven't a clue. I don't understand any of it, I'm asking
myself the same questions you are." They told him he had

to tell the police, file a complaint. He said he would do that, but the records of the Lyon police show no trace of the incident. Over the next few days, his pals asked him if there was any news; then vacation started, everyone went off in different directions, and the episode was never mentioned again. Eighteen years later, searching through Jean-Claude's past for something that might explain the tragedy, Luc remembered his friend's story. He mentioned it to the examining magistrate, who knew about it already. In one of his first interviews with the psychiatrists, the prisoner had brought it up spontaneously as an example of his mythomania: just as he'd made up a girlfriend named Claude when he was an adolescent, he'd invented the attack to draw attention to himself. "But afterward, I didn't know if it was true or false anymore. Of course I have no memory of an actual attack, I know it didn't happen, but I don't remember faking it, either—tearing my shirt or scratching myself. If I think about it, I tell myself I must have done that but I don't recall it. And I wound up believing that I'd really been attacked."

The strangest thing about this confession is that nothing obliged him to make it. After eighteen years, the story was perfectly unverifiable. It already was when he first told it to his friends, back at the nightclub. Moreover, it didn't hold together, and that's why, paradoxically, no one ever thought to doubt it. A liar usually tries to sound plausible, so what Jean-Claude was saying, which wasn't, had to be true.

. . .

WHEN I WAS IN TENTH GRADE, LOTS OF MY CLASSMATES had started smoking. At fourteen I was the smallest in the class and, afraid of being laughed at if I imitated the bigger boys, I devised a scheme. I used to pocket a cigarette from the pack of Kents my mother had bought on a trip and kept in the house in case a guest ever wanted to smoke, and at the right moment, in the café where we gathered after classes, I'd stick my hand in the pocket of my pea coat. Frowning, I'd examine my find in astonishment. In a voice that seemed painfully strident to me, I'd ask *who* had put *that* in my pocket. No one, of course, would admit having done it and, above all, no one ever paid much attention to the incident, which only I would comment on: I was certain there hadn't been a cigarette in my pocket when I left home, so somebody had slipped this one in without my noticing. I'd repeat that I didn't understand at all, as though that should put to rest any suspicion that I had arranged this little scene to make myself interesting. Well, it didn't make me interesting. My friends never refused to listen to me, but all that ever happened was that a few of them would obligingly say, "Yeah, that's weird," and then talk about something else. There I'd be, supposing I'd presented them with one of those dilemmas that, while irritating, put the mind to work. Either someone had placed that cigarette in my pocket—as I was claiming—and the question was, why? Or I was the one who'd done it, I was lying, and the question was the same: Why? What for? I used to finish up by shrugging nonchalantly and remarking that, well, since the cigarette was there, the only thing left was to smoke it. Which I'd do. But I was always puzzled and disappointed that in everyone else's eyes nothing ever seemed to have happened except the usual actions of a smoker: taking out a cigarette and lighting it, which they all did and which I wanted to do but didn't dare. It seemed that this entire little circus, this contortion through which I wanted to affirm both that I smoked and that I did so only because of highly unusual circumstances—proving that my smoking was not a personal choice I feared others might laugh at (which they wouldn't have) but an obligation arising from a mystery—was never noticed by anyone. And I can well imagine Romand's surprise at the way his friends simply accepted his unlikely explanation. He'd gone out, come back saying some guys had beaten him up, and that was that.

On the second day of the trial, when things were expected to take a decisive turn, I had breakfast with Maître Abad. He is a man my age, well-built, imperious, radiating masculine authority. I thought that Romand must have been scared witless by him but at the same time reassured at being defended by the sort of fellow who in school would have cheerfully punched his face in. Abad was devoting considerable time and energy to his defense, and without any hope of ever earning a centime: he said he was doing it in memory of the dead children.

He was worried. Romand claimed to have had a flash of memory during the night and to have suddenly recalled the *real* reason he hadn't taken his makeup exam in September 1975. I asked what that real reason was. All Abad would tell me was that if it was confirmed it would undoubtedly argue in his client's favor but that it was—alas—completely unverifiable, or rather that Romand refused to divulge the name that would allow it to be verified. Refused to divulge it, he maintained, out of respect for those close to someone who was now deceased and who had been dear to him.

"That's like those underprivileged families he was teaching to read . . ."

"Can you imagine the effect?" sighed Abad. "I told him to keep it to himself. Which reminds me, he was pleased to see you in the press section. He sends you his regards."

THERE WAS NO SENSATIONAL REVELATION. ROMAND DUTI-fully told the court the same story he'd given to the magistrate: two days before the makeup exam he had fallen down some stairs and broken his wrist. That was how, through this "ordinary accident," everything had begun. Since there is no evidence of the fall and no witness can testify whether he had his wrist bandaged in September 1975, he must have feared people would suspect he had invented the accident, either at the time or during the preliminary investigation, and he insisted that it had really happened. Then, as if once again the incoherence of his story were the guarantee of its truthfulness, he added that in fact the fall shouldn't have changed anything because one could ask to dictate the exam answers.

On the morning of the exam, the hands of his alarm clock

indicated in succession the hour when he should have gotten up, the hour when the exam began, the hour when it ended. Lying in bed, he watched the hands go around. When the exam booklets had been collected, the students gathered outside the lecture room and on café terraces to ask one another how it had gone. Early that afternoon, his parents phoned to ask him that themselves, and he told them it had gone well. No one else called him.

THREE WEEKS WENT BY BETWEEN THE DAY OF THE EXAM-ination and the posting of the test results. There was still time for him to admit that he had lied. It would have been hard for him, naturally. To this serious young man, it must have seemed impossibly painful to admit a whopping error, a childish blunder like that of Antoine Doinel in *The 400 Blows*, who extricates himself from a sticky situation at school by blurting out that his mother has just died and who then must deal with the inevitable consequences of his lies. That's the worst part: the consequences are inevitable. Unless through some miracle his mother really does die in the next twenty-four hours, the boy knows perfectly well what will follow once those forbidden words have been spoken: amazement, heartfelt commiseration, the details he'll have to cough up, thus digging himself in ever deeper, and soon the awful moment when the truth will come out. This kind of lie just happens on impulse. And as soon as it pops out, you're sorry, you dream of being able to go back one minute in time, to undo the insane mistake you just made. The most baffling thing, in Romand's case, is that he committed his folly in two stages, like the computer user who, having accidentally typed the command for erasing a valuable file, when asked by the program whether he's sure he wants to delete the file, carefully considers the pros and cons—then goes ahead and destroys it anyway. If the very childishness of his lie left him too ashamed to confess to his parents, he might still have told them he had flunked the exam. If he could no more admit a failing grade than a failure of will, he might still have sought out some university authority to explain about his broken wrist and fit of depression and to arrange for a makeup exam. Rationally speaking, anything would have been better than what he did: wait for the day the test results were posted and then announce that he had passed, that he'd been accepted as a third-year medical student.

ON THE ONE HAND LAY THE NORMAL PATH, THE WAY taken by his friends and for which he had, everyone agrees, slightly better than average qualifications. He had just stumbled on this path, but it was not too late to redeem himself, to catch up with the others: no one had seen him trip. On the other hand was the crooked road of lies you couldn't even say looked invitingly strewn with roses in contrast to the straight and narrow, which allegory always depicts as overgrown with brambles and littered with stones.

You don't need to start down the road of falsehood or go as far as the first turn to see that it's a dead end. To skip your exams and then claim you've passed them, that's not a bold bluff with some chance of success, a gambler's double or nothing: you can only get swiftly caught and expelled in shame and ridicule, which he must have feared more than anything else in the world. How could he have suspected that there was something worse than being quickly unmasked, which was *not* to be unmasked, so that this childish lie would lead him eighteen years later to murder his parents, Florence, and the children he did not yet have?

"BUT *WHY?*" ASKED THE JUDGE AT LAST.

He shrugged.

"I've asked myself that question every day for twenty years. I have no answer."

A brief silence.

"The examination results were posted, after all. You had friends. No one noticed that your name was not on the lists?"

"No. I can assure you that I didn't write it in myself. Besides, the lists were behind glass panels."

"It's a mystery."

"To me as well."

The judge leaned over toward one of her assessors, who whispered something in her ear.

Then: "It is felt that you are not really answering the question."

．　．　．

HAVING ANNOUNCED HIS SUCCESS, HE SHUT HIMSELF UP IN the studio apartment his parents had bought him, just as he had shut himself away in his bedroom as a boy after his failure at the Lycée du Parc. He spent the first trimester in the apartment without returning to Clairvaux, without going to classes, without seeing his friends again. If anyone happened to ring his doorbell, he didn't answer, waiting without moving for his visitor to give up. He'd listen to the footsteps die away down the stairs. He lay prostrate on his bed, abandoned all housekeeping, fed himself out of cans. The photocopied lecture notes cluttering his table remained open to the same page. Sometimes, the knowledge of what he had done pierced the torpor into which he was letting himself sink. What could have gotten him out of this mess? A fire at the university, burning all the exam booklets to ashes? An earthquake, destroying Lyon? His own death? I suppose he wondered why he had fucked up his life. Because he'd fucked it up royally, he was sure of that. He didn't envisage carrying on the imposture; besides, it wasn't an imposture at that point, he wasn't pretending to be a student, he had retreated from the world, holed up at home, and was waiting for it all to be over, like a criminal who knows the police will come looking for him sooner or later. He could flee, change his address, escape abroad, but no, he'd rather stay there doing nothing, rereading for the fiftieth time the same month-old newspaper, eating cold pork and beans from a can, gaining forty-five pounds, waiting for the end.

In the little group of friends he used to tag along with, there was mild surprise that never went further than vague exchanges that soon became a habit: "You seen Jean-Claude lately?" No, no one had seen him, either in classes or in the labs, and nobody had any idea what he was up to. Those most in the know talked about a romantic disappointment. Florence let them talk. And he, in his tiny apartment with the shutters closed, where he was slowly becoming a ghost—he must have taken bitter satisfaction in imagining this indifference. Perhaps, like the big baby he was, he took pleasure in the idea of dying alone in his burrow, abandoned by everyone.

But he wasn't abandoned by everyone. Shortly before the Christmas holidays, someone rang his doorbell, ringing until he opened up. It wasn't Florence. It was Luc, with his irritating energy, his complete inability to see things from any point of view except his own, but also his desire to seem like a nice guy, which made him pick up hitchhikers, lend a hand when friends were moving, and clap them on the back when they were feeling blue. We can be sure he read Jean-Claude the riot act, chewed him out for getting in a jam, told him to snap out of it—and spouted such clichés without offending Jean-Claude, who liked them himself. Both of them, during the preliminary inquiry, remembered the most intense moment of their conversation. They were driving along the Saône River; Luc was at the wheel of his car, explaining that it's when you touch bottom that you've got to give the kick that shoots you back to the surface, while Jean-Claude was listening with a glum, discouraged expression, as though he'd already gone down for the third time. Perhaps he was tempted to confess everything to Luc. How would his friend have reacted? At first, certainly, by saying something like: "Well, you've really screwed up now!" Then, always the optimist, by trying to figure out a solution, nothing unrealistic, something feasible but that involved setting things straight. Luc would have told him how to go about it, he would have organized everything, perhaps spoken to the dean of the medical school for him. It would have been easy to put oneself in Luc's hands, like a juvenile delinquent leaving everything to his lawyer. Telling Luc the truth, however, would mean debasing himself in his friend's eyes and, worse, having to face his incomprehension, the torment of his questions: "But I mean, Jean-Claude, it's crazy! Can you explain to me why on earth you did it?" That's just it, no, he couldn't explain it. He didn't feel like explaining it. He was too tired.

At a red light, Luc turned toward Jean-Claude, trying to meet his eye. He had assumed that the breakup with Florence was behind his depression (which to a certain extent was true) and had just pointed out that girls are fickle, that all was not lost. Then Jean-Claude told him he had cancer.

.   .   .

HE HADN'T INTENDED TO SAY THAT, BUT IT WAS A DAY-
dream he had been toying with for two months. A cancer
would have fixed everything. It would have excused his lie:
when you're dying, who cares if you took your second-year
finals or not? It would have brought him compassion and
admiration from Florence and all those so-called friends
who, without even realizing it, treated him as if he weren't
there. He had barely spoken the word when he felt its magic
power. He had found the answer.

The cancer he chose for himself was a lymphoma, in other
words, a capricious disease of uncertain evolution, serious
without being necessarily fatal, that doesn't prevent the suf-
ferer from leading a normal life for years at a time. In fact,
it *allowed* him to live a normal life because it took the place
of his lie, for himself and for everyone else. A few people
learned he was living with a time bomb that would one day
destroy him but that for the moment was dormant in the
secrecy of his cells—because soon he was talking about a
remission, and from that point on, no more was heard about
it. He himself, I believe, preferred to see the threat hanging
over him in this guise and to convince himself that it was
both imminent and far off, with the result that after a period
of crisis when he'd thought he was lost, reduced to waiting
for the inevitable catastrophe, he settled into the mind-set
of a patient who knows the catastrophe is unavoidable, who

knows that each moment may bring the end of the remission, but who nevertheless decides to live, to make plans, earning the admiration of those around him through his quiet courage. For him, confessing to a lymphoma instead of to an imposture meant transposing a reality that was too aberrant and personal into terms other people could understand. He would rather have suffered from a real cancer than from a lie—because lying was a disease, with its own etiology, its risks of metastasis, its guarded prognosis—but he had been fated to come down with a lie and it wasn't his fault that he had.

Life returned to normal. He went back to the university and saw his friends again, especially Florence. Quite shaken by what he had learned, Luc had asked if she knew as well, and Jean-Claude had replied with solemn delicacy that he wouldn't want that, not for the world. "You won't tell her, right? Promise me not to tell her anything," he even ventured to add, guessing that Luc, a lover of the truth, would argue: "I can't promise you that. Florence is a great girl. She has a right to know. If she found out that I knew and that I hid it from her, she'd never forgive me, and she'd be right . . ." The ploy, if it was one, worked. The girls Florence lived with suggest that she felt respect and affection for Jean-Claude but did not find him physically attractive. One of them even goes so far as to say that his flabby body disgusted her, that she couldn't stand touching him or him touching

her. The idea that she made up with him because she
believed he was seriously ill might therefore seem far-
fetched, but make up with him she did, at any rate, and two
years later they celebrated their engagement.

AN ASTONISHING SERIES OF DOCUMENTS APPEARS IN THE
case file: the correspondence between the second-year student Jean-Claude Romand and the UER/Faculté de Méde-
cine de Lyon-Nord, from 1975 to 1986. Twice, at the time
of the third-year entrance exams, he sent letters citing
reasons of health to explain his absence. These letters are
accompanied by medical certificates signed by different
practitioners who instruct him—without saying why—to
remain at home for a week or two, which happens (unfortunately) to coincide with the exam period. In 1978 the
format of the letter is the same, but "the enclosed certificate"
is not enclosed. Which occasions several follow-up letters,
to which he replies, making reference to the famous certificate as though he had already sent it in. This charade leads
to the inevitable: he is informed that he is not authorized
to present himself again in September. But he is not specifically forbidden to reregister as a second-year student, which
is what he will do regularly until 1985. Every fall, he
receives his new student ID from the registrar and, from
the examination records office, the same letter signed by the
dean of the UER forbidding him to take the third-year
entrance exam in September. It is not until November 1986

that a new department head tries to find out if it is possible to prevent this M. Romand not only from taking the exam (which he isn't doing) but also from reregistering. She is informed that the university rules make no provision for such a case. She summons the phantom student to her office; he does not show up and, no doubt alarmed by this new tone, gives no further sign of life.

IN TOUCHING ON THE DEFENDANT'S STUDENT YEARS, THE prosecution and the defense confessed to being equally astonished, and Romand shared their amazement. "It surprised me, too," he said, "that I could get away with that." In a pinch he might have gambled on the sheer unwieldiness of the bureaucracy, deluded himself that he was a mere number, but he never imagined that he would register as a second-year medical student for twelve years in a row. In any case, the alarm should have gone off much sooner among those for whom he wasn't a number but Jean-Claude the friend, Jean-Claude the fiancé. As it happened, nothing happened. He attended classes, used the university library. On the table in his apartment he had the same textbooks and photocopied lectures as the other students and he continued to lend his notes to those less conscientious than he was. He spent as much time and energy pretending to become a doctor as he would have to become one in reality. After he and Florence became a couple again, they fell into the habit of cramming for exams together, asking each other practice test questions. They weren't taking the same courses any-more, however, because Florence had failed her second-year final, the one he was supposed to have passed, and like their friend Jacques Cottin, as well as the two girls who shared her apartment, she had fallen back on pharmacology. She'd been somewhat disappointed, without making a fuss about it: better to be a good pharmacist than a bad doctor, and Jean-Claude would make a good doctor—and perhaps some-thing more. He was ambitious, a hard worker, someone all his friends thought would go far. She helped him study for his board exam and he helped her with the pharmacology curriculum. All in all, he completed the entire course of medical studies, except that he didn't take the exams or participate in the clinical training. For the exams, he some-times put in an appearance at the beginning and the end of the session, counting on the crowd and everyone's nervousness to mask his absence in the meantime. For the clinical courses, the classes were smaller and each student was personally supervised by a specialist, so it was impos-sible to slip in on the sly, but since the training took place at various hospitals in the Lyon area, he could claim he was doing his someplace other than the one where the person he was talking to was assigned. One can imagine what even the clumsiest comedy writer could do with such a plot, the scenes where the imposter finds himself trapped between two people to whom he has told different stories. Neither Romand nor his classmates can recall any such scenes, however, so we'll have to assume that they never occurred.

THEIR FRIENDS WERE STARTING TO GET MARRIED. JEAN-Claude and Florence were much in demand as witnesses. No one doubted that it would soon be their turn. Florence's parents were urging them to take the plunge—they adored their future son-in-law. It was in their house near Annecy that the wedding was celebrated, in the presence of 150 guests. The following year Florence defended her thesis in pharmacology, earning high commendation, while Jean-Claude passed the medical board examination in Paris. At first a research assistant at INSERM (the National Institute of Health and Medical Research) in Lyon, he was then assigned to the World Health Organization in Geneva as a research scientist. The couple moved from Lyon to Ferney-Voltaire, where Luc Ladmiral had just taken over his father's medical practice, and Jacques Cottin a pharmacy where Florence would be able to work part-time. Annecy was only an hour's drive to the south, Clairvaux the same distance to the north. They had the pleasures of the countryside, the mountains, and the Swiss capital at their doorstep; an international airport; an open and cosmopolitan society. Lastly, it was ideal for children.

Their friends were starting families. Jean-Claude and

Florence were much in demand as godparents. No one doubted that it would soon be their turn. Jean-Claude doted on his goddaughter Sophie, the first child of Luc and Cécile, who were already on their second. Caroline Romand was born on May 14, 1985, Antoine on February 2, 1987. Their father brought them magnificent gifts sent by his bosses at WHO and INSERM, who did not forget the children's birthdays later on. Florence, who had never met these people, wrote thank-you letters her husband promised to deliver.

Most of the Romand family photo albums were destroyed when their house burned, but a few pictures were saved, and they look just like any of ours. Jean-Claude was no different from me, Luc, or any other young father: he bought a camera when his daughter was born and eagerly photographed Caroline and Antoine as babies—their bottles, their games in the playpen, their first steps, Florence's smile as she bent over her children. She in turn took pictures of him, so proud to be carrying them, tossing them in his arms, giving them their bath. In these snapshots he wears a look of goofy wonderment that must have touched his wife and persuaded her she had made the right choice after all, that of loving a man who loved them like this, her and their children.

Their children.

He called Florence "Flo," Caroline "Caro," and Antoine "Titou." He frequently used possessive pronouns: my Flo, my Caro, my Titou. And often, with that affectionate mockery inspired in us by the solemn dignity of toddlers, he would say "Monsieur Titou." So, Monsieur Titou, did we have a good sleep?

HE SAYS: "THE SOCIAL PART WAS FALSE, BUT THE EMO-tional part was true." He says that he was a fake doctor but a real husband and father, that he loved his wife and children with all his heart, and that they loved him, too. Those who knew them insist, even now, that Caroline and Antoine were happy, confident, well-adjusted; she was a trifle shy, while he was full of fun. Their class photos from the case file show him grinning ear to ear and missing a few baby teeth. They say that children always know everything, that you can't hide anything from them, and I'm the first to believe it. I take another look at the photos. I'm not sure.

THEY WERE PROUD THAT THEIR FATHER WAS A DOCTOR. "The doctor takes care of sick people," wrote Caroline in a school composition. He didn't take care of them in the classic sense of the word, didn't even take care of his own family—they were all, himself included, Luc's patients—and he claimed never to have written a prescription in his life. But as Florence explained, he invented the medicines that allow people to be taken care of, which made him a superdoctor. The adults didn't know much more about his work than the children. If questioned, casual acquaintances might have said that he had an important job at WHO and traveled a lot; close friends might have added that his research was on arteriosclerosis, that he taught at the University of Dijon, that he dealt with important political figures like Laurent Fabius (the former prime minister and current president of the National Assembly)—but he never spoke of these things himself, and any mention of his impressive connections in front of him seemed rather to embarrass him. He was, as Florence put it, "very compartmentalized," strictly separating his personal and professional relations, never inviting his colleagues from WHO to his house, refusing to allow himself to be disturbed at home by anyone from his office, or at work by any of his family or friends. Moreover, nobody had his office phone number, not even his wife, who contacted him through an answering service operated by the telephone company: you left a message in a voice mailbox, which sent him a signal on the beeper he always carried with him, and then he quickly called back. Neither his wife nor anyone else found the arrangement strange. It was one of his personality traits, like his gruffness, which she often joked about: "One of these days, I'm going to find out my husband's a Communist spy."

The family, including his and Florence's parents, was the center of his life. Around it gravitated a small circle of intimates: the Ladmirals, the Cottins, and a few other couples with whom Florence had struck up a friendship. Like the Romands, these people were in their thirties; they had similar professions, similar incomes, and children the same age. They were informal with one another, going to restaurants and movies together, usually in Geneva, sometimes in Lyon or Lausanne. The Ladmirals remember going with the Romands to see a few hit movies, some Béjart ballets for which Jean-Claude had gotten tickets through WHO, and Valérie Lemercier's stand-up comedy show, but also a play by Bernard-Marie Koltès that Luc would describe in his deposition as "an endless dialogue between two people picking cotton about how hard their lives are, which several friends who went with us couldn't figure out at all." As for Jean-Claude, he had enjoyed it, which didn't surprise the others, who considered him an intellectual. He read a great deal and was partial to semiphilosophical essays by famous scientists, things like *Chance and Necessity* by Jacques Monod. He claimed to be a rationalist and an agnostic, although he respected his wife's faith and admitted that their children even attended a religious school: they would be free, later on, to choose for themselves. He admired Mother Teresa and Brigitte Bardot, Bernard Kouchner and the activist priest Father Pierre. He was among the significant percentage of

French citizens who think that if Jesus were to reappear among us it would be as a humanitarian doctor. Kouchner was his friend, Bardot had given him a signed bust of herself as Marianne, the spirit of the French Republic. A supporter of animal rights, he had joined her foundation, as well as the SPCA, Greenpeace, Handicap International, but also the conservative Club Perspectives et Réalités de Bellegarde, the golf club of Divonne-les-Bains, and the Automobile-Club Médical—thanks to which he'd obtained a caduceus to stick on his car's windshield. The investigators found evidence of a few donations and subscriptions to these organizations, whose bulletins, badges, and stickers he left lying around. There were also a rubber stamp and some business cards in the name of Dr. Jean-Claude Romand, Fellow of the French College of Physicians, but he wasn't listed in any professional directory. All it took, the day after the fire, was a few phone calls to bring that facade crashing down. Throughout the preliminary investigation the judge repeatedly expressed astonishment that such calls had not been made earlier, not out of malice or suspicion but simply because, even if you are "very compartmentalized," to work for ten years without your wife or friends ever calling you at the office is simply unheard of. It's impossible to think about this story without feeling that there is a mystery here with a hidden explanation. But the mystery is that there is no explanation and that, as unlikely as it may seem, that's how it happened.

· · ·

IN THE MORNINGS, HE WAS THE ONE WHO DROVE THE
children to the Ecole Saint-Vincent. He would accompany
them into the courtyard, exchange a few words with the
teachers or the students' mothers (who held up as an example
to their husbands this father who was so close to his children), then drive off toward Geneva. It's a little over a mile
to the border, crossed twice a day by the several thousand
residents of the Gex region who work in Switzerland. Like
commuters on a suburban train, they have regular schedules;
they greet one another and the customs officers who wave
them through without inspection. Many are international
civil servants, and when they enter the city, instead of turning right toward the business district and the Cornavin railroad station, they go left toward the botanical garden and
the residential neighborhood where their organizations have
their headquarters. Romand joined this stream of traffic,
cruising along the wide and placid green avenues, more
often than not winding up in the parking lot of WHO.
Entering with a visitor's badge, carrying a briefcase, he followed a familiar orbit, going from the ground-floor library
to the conference rooms and the publications office, where
he systematically swept up anything printed and free: his
house and car overflowed with papers bearing the letterhead
or stamp of WHO. He used all the services offered by the
organization—a post office where he sent his mail, a bank
where he made most of his withdrawals, a travel agency

through which he planned the family vacations—but did not risk going upstairs, where security guards might have asked him what he was looking for. Did he at least once, taking advantage of momentarily deserted halls, visit the office with the window marked by an X on the photo of the building he'd given his parents? Did he look outside, his forehead pressed against the glass, at what there was to see from that window? Did he sit in *his* chair, did he walk by the fellow coming back to sit there, did he call him on his direct line? He says no, the thought never even crossed his mind. His mother-in-law remembers that one Sunday when the whole family had gone to Switzerland, the children had wanted to see Papa's office, so Papa had agreed to the detour. They'd pulled into the parking lot, he'd pointed out the window. And that's all.

In the beginning he went to WHO every day, later on less regularly. Instead of the road to Geneva, he'd take the one to Gex and Divonne or the one to Bellegarde that leads to the freeway and Lyon. He'd stop at a newsstand to buy an armful of papers: dailies, magazines, scientific journals. Then he'd go read them, either in a café—he was careful to change cafés often and to choose them far enough from home—or in his car. He would park in a lot or at a highway rest stop and stay there for hours, reading, taking notes, dozing. He'd have a sandwich for lunch and continue reading throughout the afternoon in a different café, at a different rest stop. When this routine became too monotonous, he'd stroll around Bourg-en-Bresse, Bellegarde, Gex, Nantua, and especially Lyon, where he visited his favorite bookstores, FNAC and Flammarion on the Place Bellecour. Other days, he needed open air and nature and would drive into the Jura Mountains. He followed the winding road that leads to the pass of La Faucille, where there is an inn called the Wood Grouse. Florence and the children liked to go there on Sundays to ski and eat French fries. During the week it was deserted. He'd have a glass of wine, go walking in the forest. From the crest of the mountain one can see the countryside around Gex, Lake Geneva, and, on a clear day, the Alps. Spread out before him was the civilized plain where Dr. Romand and others like him lived; behind him were the narrow valleys and dark forests where he'd spent his lonely childhood. On Thursdays, when he taught a course in Dijon, he would visit his parents, who were delighted to show off to their neighbors this great big son who was so important, so busy, but always ready to go out of his way to give them a hug and a kiss. His father's sight was failing; toward the end he was almost blind and could no longer walk alone in the forest. Jean-Claude would go with him, holding on to his arm, listening to him talk about the trees and his captivity in Germany. After their walk, they would go over the notebooks in which Aimé, who for a long time had been informally providing information to a weather station, had been recording the high and low temperatures every day for forty years, the way other people keep a private diary.

Lastly, there were the trips—conferences, seminars, symposiums, all over the world. He would buy a guide to the country; Florence would pack his suitcase. He'd drive off in his car, which he would supposedly leave in the long-term lot at the Geneva airport. In a comfortable hotel room, often near the airport, he would take off his shoes, stretch out on the bed, spend three or four days watching television and the planes taking off and landing outside his window. He studied the guidebooks so he wouldn't make any mistakes in his stories when he got home. He telephoned his family every day to tell them what time it was and what the weather was like in São Paulo or Tokyo. He'd ask how things were going while he was gone. He'd tell his wife, his children, his parents that he missed them, was thinking of them, sent them a big kiss. He phoned no one else: whom would he have called? After a few days, he went home with presents bought in an airport gift shop. Everyone made a fuss over him. He was tired from jet lag.

DIVONNE IS A SMALL SPA NEAR THE SWISS BORDER BEST known for its casino. I once used it as a setting for a few pages of a novel about a woman who lives a double life and tries to lose herself in the world of gambling. The novel was meant to be realistic and well-documented but, since I hadn't visited all the casinos I wrote about, I put Divonne on the shores of Lake Geneva when it's really about six miles away. There is actually something there referred to as a lake, but it's only a small sheet of water next to the lot where Romand often parked. I parked there, too. It's the clearest memory I've kept of my first visit to the landscape of his life. There were only two other cars, unoccupied. It was windy. I reread the letter he'd sent me with directions, I looked at the water, looked up at the gray sky to follow the flight of birds whose name I didn't know—I can't identify birds or trees and I find that sad. It was chilly. I started the engine to get some heat. The hot air made me sleepy. I thought about the studio where I go every morning after driving my children to school. This studio exists, people can visit me and phone me there. That's where I write and piece together screenplays that usually get filmed. But I know what it's like to spend all one's days unobserved: the hours passed staring at the ceiling, the fear of no longer existing. I wondered what he felt in his car. Pleasure? A mocking exultation at the idea of so masterfully fooling everyone around him? No; I was sure of that. Anguish? Did he imagine how it would all end, in what way the truth would come out, what would happen next? Did he weep, resting his head on the steering wheel? Or didn't he feel anything at all? Was he, in his solitude, becoming a machine that drove, walked, read, without really thinking or feeling, a residual and anesthetized Dr. Romand? A lie usually serves to conceal a truth, something shameful, perhaps, but real. His concealed nothing. Behind the false Dr. Romand there was no real Jean-Claude Romand.

I remembered a film that was a big success at that time. It told the story—a legend for a time of economic crisis—of a laid-off executive who doesn't dare tell the truth to his wife and children. He'd thought he would quickly find a new job and now he's already at the end of his benefits. Every morning he leaves, every evening he comes home, pretending he has been to the office and back. He spends his days wandering around, avoiding his neighborhood. He doesn't speak to anyone, every face frightens him because it could belong to a former colleague, a friend who would wonder what the hell he was doing on a park bench in the middle of the afternoon . . . But one day he meets some men in a similar situation, rowdy guys with plenty of expertise in hard times and homelessness. With them he discovers a world that is harsher but warmer and more alive than the one in which he was cozily vegetating before his free fall. He becomes more mature and more human: the film has a happy ending.

Romand told me that he'd seen the film on television with Florence, who hadn't found it at all disturbing and had, in fact, enjoyed it. He knew that his story could not have a happy ending. He never confided or tried to confide his secret—not to his wife, or his best friend, or a stranger on a bench, or a prostitute, or any of those good souls whose job it is to listen and understand—priest, psychotherapist, the anonymous ear of a suicide hotline. In eighteen years of living a double life, he never met anyone, spoke to anyone, mixed with any of those parallel societies like the worlds of gambling, drugs, or the night, where he might have been able to feel less alone. Neither did he ever actually try to pretend he was a doctor. When he made his entrance on the domestic stage of his life, everyone thought he was coming from another stage where he played another role, that of the big shot who travels the world, associates with government ministers, dines in official splendor, a role he would resume when he went out the door again. But there was no other stage, no other audience for whom he played the other role. Outside, he found himself naked. He returned to absence, a void, a blank that wasn't an incidental accident but the sole experience of his life. He had never known any other, I believe, even before that life split in two.

Until the end of his studies, he was supported by his parents, who had bought him a studio apartment in Lyon and a car, preferring to sell a few cuts of timber rather than see their son waste his time baby-sitting or giving private lessons to eke out his pocket money. The moment of truth should have arrived when, having finished medical school and gotten married, he joined the workaday world as a researcher at INSERM. Nothing happened. He continued to draw on his parents' bank accounts, to which he had legal access. He considered their assets his own and they encouraged him in this, unperturbed to see their savings regularly tapped by a son who was surely earning a good living. When he left Lyon for the Gex region, he sold the studio for 300,000 francs, which he kept. Once he was at WHO, he said or let it be understood that as an international civil servant he was in a position to make extremely advantageous investments at a rate of 18 percent, an opportunity he could share with his family. The Romands were not the kind of people to cheat on their taxes by putting their savings into Swiss banks, but as it was their son's idea, that was enough for them. Watching their nest egg shrink with each succeeding bank statement, instead of worrying they blessed Jean-Claude for managing—in spite of his many duties—their little pensioners' portfolio. Their confidence was shared by Uncle Claude, who besides his garage had some shares in the timber company managed by his brother and who also entrusted his nephew with a few tens of thousands of francs, persuaded that provided the sum was left untouched, it would multiply tenfold.

Romand lived on that at the beginning of his marriage. Florence declared to the income tax authorities the very modest salary she earned by temporarily filling in for pharmacists in the area, and he declared no income because since he worked in Switzerland he had—he said—no taxes to pay. Once she'd signed their joint return, he would add, "Profession: student," sending along a copy of his card. They drove an old Volvo, visited their parents for vacations, occasionally spent ten days in Spain or Italy. Their two-room apartment, 538 square feet at two thousand francs a month, was suitable for a young couple, less suitable for a young couple with a child, and not suitable at all for a family of four, especially when Florence's mother would come visit for a few weeks. It became a standing joke with their friends, who one after the other bought or built houses while the Romands stubbornly camped out on their sofa beds like perpetual students.

"You're earning how much?" Luc started in on him one day. "Thirty, forty thousand francs, something like that?" (He'd tossed out this figure as though it were obvious, and Jean-Claude had nodded in confirmation.) "I mean, really, you could afford something better. Otherwise people will end up thinking you're a cheapskate or else that you've got an expensive mistress!" Everyone laughed, Florence loudest of all, while Jean-Claude shrugged, muttering that they weren't necessarily staying in the area for a long time, he might take a position abroad, and that moving again now would drive him nuts. He also said he was disgusted by all the easy money floating around the Gex area; he had no desire to follow the crowd, to raise his children according to such values, and he made it a point of honor to live modestly. The two explanations, laziness and virtue, were not contradictory, bolstering on the contrary the image of the scholar indifferent to material things. The question, though, was if Florence was as indifferent as her husband. In fact, despite her simple tastes and her confidence in Jean-Claude, she found what their friends said quite reasonable and urged him to find a bigger place for the family. He was evasive, put the question off, didn't have time to think about it. He was already finding it difficult to make ends meet.

The year Antoine was born, Florence's father retired from his job in Annecy. A disguised downsizing, his retirement brought him a bonus of 400,000 francs. It's most unlikely that Jean-Claude offered openly to invest the money; he must have spoken to Florence, who spoke to her mother, who spoke to her husband, so that Jean-Claude found himself in the convenient position of being asked instead of having to ask himself. He agreed to do his father-in-law a favor by investing 378,000 francs for him at the UOB, a Geneva bank with headquarters on the Quai des Bergues. This sum was obviously deposited in an account in Jean-Claude's name, since he was the one whose position entitled him to make such an investment. Pierre Crolet's name does not appear on any document. Generally speaking, neither the Crolets nor the elder Romands, the principle investors, ever saw a bank statement confirming the deposit of their funds or the interest accrued. But what could be safer than a Swiss bank—unless it's a Swiss bank to which one has access through Jean-Claude Romand? They thought their money was working quietly on the Quai des Bergues and they had no wish to interrupt this work. At least that's what Jean-Claude was counting on until the day his father-in-law told him he wanted to withdraw a portion of his capital so that he could buy himself a Mercedes. His wife was well taken care of, his children were off on their own; why deprive himself of this pleasure?

A few weeks later, on October 23, 1988, Pierre Crolet fell on the stairs of his home where he was alone with his son-in-law and died just before the arrival of the paramedics.

AFTER THE FIRE, A NEW INVESTIGATION WAS ORDERED AT the request of the Crolet family. Of course, it uncovered nothing. At the trial, the prosecutor claimed that it was impossible to silence the terrible misgivings with which the Crolets, who certainly didn't need that burden, continued to live. Abad jumped up to accuse the prosecution of fabricating new charges against his client, who didn't need that burden either. At the end of the proceedings, before the court retired to deliberate, the accused insisted on telling the Crolet family, as God was his witness, that he had had no hand in his father-in-law's death. He added that he believed there was no forgiveness for unconfessed sins. Short of a confession on his part someday, we will never learn any more and I have no hypothesis to offer. I only wish to add that during one of his first interrogations he told the examining magistrate, "If I'd killed him, I would say so. One more wouldn't make any difference."

By simply saying no, he didn't kill his father-in-law, he takes advantage of the presumption of innocence. By swearing it before God, he introduces a dimension that may be convincing or not, depending on how one feels. But saying that one more death doesn't change anything and that if he'd done it he would confess it—that ignores or pretends to ignore the enormous difference between monstrous but irrational crimes and a sordid crime. It's true that it doesn't change much from a punitive point of view since the death penalty has been abolished in France. But morally—or, if one prefers, with regard to the image that he projects of himself and that is important to him—it's not at all the same to be the agent of a tragedy, impelled by some obscure fate to commit acts arousing pity and terror, or to be a petty crook who cautiously chooses as dupes the elderly and trusting members of his own family and who to save himself shoves his father-in-law down the stairs. Now, even if this crime is unproven, the rest is true: Romand is *also* a petty crook and it is much harder for him to admit to that, because it is sordid and shameful, than it is to confess crimes so outrageous that they confer tragic stature on him. In a way, *this* has served to conceal *that*, without completely succeeding.

ANOTHER DISTRESSING EVENT TOOK PLACE AT ABOUT THE same time. Pierre Crolet's sister, Florence's aunt, had a husband suffering from an incurable cancer. She testified at the trial that Jean-Claude spoke to her one day about a cure he was in the last stages of developing with his supervisor at WHO, a treatment involving fresh cells from embryos harvested at an abortion clinic. This cure could arrest, perhaps reverse, the disease; unfortunately it was not yet commercially available, so there was a good chance the uncle might die before he could be cured. Having hooked the aunt, Romand supposedly then explained that he might be able to obtain one or two doses, but that the production cost, at that stage of the research, was quite high: fifteen thousand francs a capsule, and two were required for the initial treatment. It was decided to go ahead anyway. A few months later, after the uncle had undergone a serious operation, another double dose was required, which brought the cost of the cure to sixty thousand francs in cash. Since the outcome of the treatment was so uncertain, the patient at first refused to dip heavily into the savings account he planned to leave his widow, but then he let himself be persuaded. He died the following year.

Confronted with this damning testimony from someone who was still alive, physically present, and able to contradict him, which was an unusual situation during his trial, Romand replied in an increasing panic that (1) the idea of the miracle treatment came not from him but from Florence, who'd heard about it (where? from whom?); (2) he hadn't presented it as a miracle treatment but as a placebo that, even if it didn't do any good, certainly wouldn't do any harm (then why was it so expensive?); (3) he'd never claimed to have been involved in its development, never invoked the authority of his superior at WHO, and anyway a woman as well-informed as Florence would never for a second have believed that a high-level scientist would illicitly sell cancer cures still under development (this well-informed woman had believed things that were even more unbelievable); (4) he was only an intermediary who met with a researcher at the Cornavin railroad station and gave him the money in exchange for the capsules (pressed for particulars about the researcher, he said he didn't remember his name, he must have written it down at the time in his notebook, which, as bad luck would have it, had burned up in the fire). Faced with the evidence, he defended himself like the person who borrows the caldron in one of Freud's favorite stories: reproached by the lender for having returned it with a hole in the bottom, the borrower declares first that the caldron had no hole when he returned it, then that the hole was already there when he borrowed it, lastly that he'd never borrowed a caldron from anyone.

WHAT IS INDISPUTABLE IS THAT THE DEATH OF HIS FATHER-in-law was providential for Romand. To begin with, there was no longer any question of touching the money in the Swiss account. Then Mme. Crolet decided to sell the house, now too large for her on her own, and handed over to her son-in-law the proceeds of that sale, which amounted to 1.3 million francs. In the months following the accident, he was a pillar of strength for the bereaved, who now considered him the head of the family. He was only thirty-four years old, but his calm and thoughtful maturity had prepared him for this moment when one ceases to be a son and becomes a father, not only to one's children but also to one's own parents, who are gently slipping into their second childhood. He played that role in his own family and now for his mother-in-law, too, who had been plunged into depression by grief. Florence had been hit hard as well. Hoping to distract her, he decided to abandon their little apartment for Prévessin, near Ferney, where they rented a renovated farmhouse more in keeping with their social position, a home she would enjoy fixing up.

Things began happening at a faster pace. He fell in love.

Rémi Hourtin was a psychiatrist; his wife, Corinne, a child psychologist. They had opened an office together in Geneva and rented an apartment in Ferney above the Ladmirals, who introduced them to their circle of friends. At first everyone found them funny, lively, a touch pretentious. Pretty, probably lacking in self-confidence, and clearly eager to seem captivating, Corinne displayed naive admiration or cruel contempt for things, always in slavish conformity with the decrees of women's magazines on what was in or out. Rémi had a taste for fancy restaurants, racy remarks, cigars and clear fruit brandies at the end of a meal, a lavish lifestyle. The Ladmirals felt and still feel for this jolly companion the indulgent affection people with tidy lives have for fast-lane types who faithfully keep playing their parts.

Romand must have envied and perhaps secretly hated Rémi's glib tongue, his success with women, his relaxed, uncomplicated approach to life.

It quickly became obvious that the Hourtins were having their troubles and that each of them took liberties that were frowned on in that corner of the world. They had about them a shocking air of amorality. Luc, a handsome man and not insensitive to Corinne's charm, was able to catch himself in time, but this aborted adventure along with others that doubtless went further earned the young woman a reputation as a man-eater and homewrecker. When she left Rémi to move to Paris with their two little girls, their friends took the side of the abandoned husband. Only Florence Romand pointed out that Rémi must have cheated on his wife as much as she had on him, that if they'd made mistakes it was their own business, and that she, Florence, having never suffered any hurt from them, did not wish to judge either of them and would remain friends with both. She often phoned Corinne, and when she and Jean-Claude spent a few days in Paris, they all had dinner together. The Romands visited the apartment Corinne had found near the Eglise d'Auteuil in the sixteenth arrondissement and showed her pictures of the house they themselves were about to move into. Corinne was touched by their kindness and loyalty. At the same time, this tall, athletic girl and her big teddy bear of a husband belonged to a closed chapter in her life: she'd crossed off the province, its malicious gossip, its petty compromises, and now she was struggling to make a life for herself and her children in Paris. She and her visitors no longer had much to say to one another.

Three weeks later she was astonished to receive an impressive bouquet of flowers with Jean-Claude's card saying that he was in Paris for a conference and would be delighted to invite her out that evening. He was at the Hôtel Royal Monceau. This detail as well surprised Corinne, and favorably: she wouldn't have imagined he was used to staying in four-star hotels. He continued to surprise her, first by treating her to a fine restaurant and not a simple brasserie, then by talking about himself, his career, his research. She knew he was quite reserved on those subjects—it was a characteristic as proverbial as Rémi's fondness for jokes—but seeing him as nothing more than a serious and somewhat dull scientist like so many others in the Gex region, she had never tried to break through that reserve. Suddenly she discovered a different man, a researcher of great ability and international reputation, on familiar terms with Bernard Kouchner. Soon he might be taking over the direction of INSERM—he mentioned that in passing, making it clear that he was wavering because of the burden of additional work involved. The contrast between this new reality and his earlier lackluster image made him seem all the more appealing. It's common knowledge that the most remarkable men are also the most modest, the least concerned with others' opinions of them. This was the first time Corinne, who had known mostly seductive sensualists like her ex-husband, had formed a friendship with one of these remarkable men, austere scholars or tormented geniuses whom she had admired from afar until then, as though they lived only in the arts and sciences pages of the newspapers.

He came back, invited her out to dinner again, spoke to her some more about his research and his conferences. The second time, however, before saying good night, he announced that he had something a bit delicate to say: he was in love with her.

Familiar with the desires of men, Corinne had been flattered that he'd chosen her as his friend without any ulterior motive of making her his mistress: that meant he was truly interested in her. Discovering she'd been mistaken, she was at first stunned (in spite of all her experience, she hadn't seen it coming), then disappointed (he was just like the rest of them), a bit disgusted (she didn't find him at all physically attractive), and finally moved by the pleading note in his confession. She had no trouble gently turning him down.

The next day he telephoned to apologize for his badly timed declaration, and before she got home from work he dropped a package off at her place containing a ring of yellow gold with an emerald surrounded by little diamonds (19,200 francs from the jeweler Victoroff). She called to tell him he was crazy, she would never accept such a gift. He insisted. She kept it.

He fell into the habit, that spring, of spending a day and night in Paris every week. Arriving from Geneva on the 12:15 flight, he would check into the Royal Monceau or the Concorde La Fayette and invite Corinne out that evening to a fancy restaurant. He explained these trips by claiming to be doing important experimental work at the Institut Pasteur. He used this pretext with Florence as well. In deceiving the two of them, he could tell the same lie.

THESE WEEKLY DINNERS WITH CORINNE BECAME THE great affair of his life. It was like a spring welling up in the desert, something miraculous and unexpected. He no longer thought about anything but that, about what he would tell her and what she would say in return. The words that had whirled around in his head for so long—he was finally saying them to someone. Before, when he left home at the wheel of his car, he knew that until he returned he would be lost on a vast beach of dead and empty time where he wouldn't speak to anyone, wouldn't exist for anyone. Now, this time preceded and followed the moment of seeing Corinne again. It separated him from her and drew him nearer to her. It was alive, rich with expectation, uncertainty, and hope. Arriving at the hotel, he knew he was going to telephone her, arrange to see her that evening, have flowers sent to her. Shaving in front of the mirror, in the luxurious bathroom at the Royal Monceau, he saw the face she would see.

He had known Corinne in the world he shared with others, but with one bold stroke, by inviting her and establishing the ritual of these tête-à-têtes, he had introduced her into the other world, the one where he had always been alone but where for the first time he wasn't anymore, where for the first time he existed in someone else's eyes. He was still the only one to know this, however. He reminded himself of the unhappy monster in *Beauty and the Beast*, with the added touch that the beauty had no idea she was dining with him inside a castle where no one else before her had ever gone. She thought she was sitting across from a normal inhabitant of the normal world, a world in which he seemed remarkably involved, and she could not imagine—psychologist though she was—that one could be so radically and secretly estranged from it.

Did he almost tell her the truth? Away from her, he cherished the hope that next time, another time, the words of his confession would finally be spoken. And that it would go well, that there would be a flow of confided secrets, a mysterious understanding between them that would allow the words to be spoken. For hours on end, he rehearsed the preliminaries. Perhaps he could recount his strange story as if it had happened to someone else—a complex and tortured individual, a psychological case, a hero in a novel. As he spoke, his voice would grow more and more solemn (he was afraid that in reality it would become increasingly shrill).

His voice would caress Corinne, envelop her in his emotion. In control of himself until then, expertly dominating every situation, the fabulist would become human, fragile. His weak spot was now revealed. He had met a woman. He loved her. Not daring to tell her the truth, he would rather die than continue lying to her. Corinne gazed at him intently. She took his hand. Tears ran down their cheeks. They went up to their room in silence, they were naked, weeping, they made love, and their shared tears tasted of deliverance. Now he could die, it wasn't important anymore, nothing was important anymore, he was forgiven, saved.

These reveries filled his lonely thoughts. During the day in his car, at night next to his sleeping wife, he created a Corinne who understood him, forgave him, consoled him. But in his heart he knew that if he were face-to-face with her, things could not turn out this way. To move and impress her, his story would have had to be different, something like what the investigators would imagine three years later. As a fake doctor but real spy, real drug trafficker, real terrorist, he would surely have fascinated her. As simply a fake doctor, mired in fear and humdrum routine, swindling humble retirees with cancer, he didn't have a chance, and it wasn't Corinne's fault. Maybe she was superficial and full of preconceived ideas, but even if she hadn't been so shallow, it wouldn't have changed a thing. No woman would agree to embrace that Beast, who would never be transformed into Prince Charming. No woman could love what he really was.

He wondered whether there was a more unspeakable truth in the whole world, wondered if other men were so ashamed of themselves. Perhaps certain sexual perverts, the ones they call short eyes in prisons, the ones other criminals despise and mistreat.

SINCE HE WAS WORKING AND TRAVELING A GREAT DEAL, Florence took care of their move to Prévessin by herself. She arranged everything, decorated the house in her own warm and unpretentious style (pine shelves, rattan armchairs, duvets in gay colors), and hung a swing in the garden for the children. He, usually so careful with their money, began signing checks without even listening to her explanations. He bought himself a Range Rover. She never suspected either that the money came from her mother's house or that he was spending it in Paris with even greater abandon. There was much astonishment over this at the trial, but while they did have a joint account, it seems she never looked at their bank statements.

As for the Ladmirals, they were building a house a few miles away, out in the countryside. They were living in the midst of the construction, half in their old house, half in the new one. Pregnant again, Cécile was supposed to rest as much as possible. Luc remembers Jean-Claude dropping by unexpectedly at the beginning of the summer. The workers had just left after pouring the concrete slab for the terrace. Luc and his visitor had a beer out in the rubble-strewn garden. Luc was preoccupied with the worries of a man dealing with a contractor. He inspected the work site, talking about delays, cost overruns, the placement of the outdoor grill, topics that obviously bored Jean-Claude. Not wishing to dwell on such problems, Luc dutifully asked Jean-Claude about his own move to Prévessin, but that didn't interest him either, nor did the week's vacation he'd just spent in Greece with Florence and the children. He answered distractedly, smiled with a distant, evasive air, as if he were pursuing an inner reverie that was infinitely seductive. Luc suddenly realized that he'd lost weight, looked younger, and instead of his usual tweed jacket and corduroy trousers was wearing a well-cut and expensive-looking suit. Luc had the vague feeling that if Cécile had been there, she would have understood at a glance. As if to confirm Luc's suspicion, Jean-Claude blurted out that he might be moving to Paris soon. For professional reasons, naturally. Luc pointed out that he'd just moved to Prévessin. Of course, of course, but that didn't mean he couldn't rent a pied-à-terre and come back to the house on weekends. Luc shrugged: "I hope you're not doing anything foolish."

Late one evening the following week Jean-Claude telephoned him from the airport in Geneva. His voice was thick. He didn't feel well, he was afraid he was having a coronary, but he didn't want to go to the hospital. He could drive, and he was on his way. A half hour later, pale, extremely agitated, wheezing heavily, he came through the front door, which had been left ajar so that he wouldn't awaken everyone. Luc examined him and diagnosed a simple panic attack. They sat down facing each other, like the old friends they were, in the dimly lighted living room. It was a quiet night; Cécile and the children were sleeping upstairs. "So, okay," said Luc, "what's going on?"

If Jean-Claude, as he told it, was on the verge of spilling the whole truth that night, his listener's first reaction made him beat a retreat. Luc blew up over his having a mistress. And that it was Corinne outraged him. He'd never had a very high opinion of her; what he was hearing confirmed his suspicions. But Jean-Claude! Jean-Claude, cheating on Florence! It was the collapse of a cathedral. Although this was rather unflattering to his friend, Luc assumed that Jean-Claude was the decent guy, fairly inexperienced in love, and Corinne the siren who through sheer malice, to confirm her power and destroy a home she envied, was ensnaring him in her net. That's what happened when you didn't sow your wild oats at twenty—you wound up pushing forty in a full-blown fit of adolescence. Jean-Claude tried to protest, to seem not ashamed but proud of his adventure, to appear in Luc's eyes as that dashing Dr. Romand whose reflection shone from the mirrors of the Royal Monceau. A waste of time. Luc made him promise, in the end, to break off the affair as soon as possible and then tell Florence everything, because silence is a couple's worst enemy. A crisis weathered together, however, can turn out to be their strongest ally. If

Jean-Claude didn't act or delayed too long, he, Luc, would speak to Florence about it for both their sakes.

LUC DID NOT HAVE TO SHOW HIS DEVOTION BY DENOUNC-ing Jean-Claude to his wife. In mid-August, Jean-Claude and Corinne spent three days together in Rome. He had insisted on the trip, which was a nightmare for her. Their accounts, equally elliptical, agree on this point: on the last day, she told him she didn't love him, because she found him too sad. "Too sad": those are the words they both used. He wept, pleaded the way he had fifteen years earlier with Florence, and like Florence, she was kind to him. They parted promising always to remain friends.

He rejoined his family, on vacation in Clairvaux. Early one morning, he drove into the woods of Saint-Maurice. His father, who had been a forester there, had shown him a chasm where a fall would be fatal. He says that he tried to jump in, that he did jump in but was held back by branches that scratched his face and tore his clothes. He did not succeed in dying but doesn't know how he got out of there alive, either. He drove as far as Lyon, checked into a hotel, and phoned Florence to tell her he'd just had an accident on the freeway between Geneva and Lausanne. He'd been thrown from the car, a Mercedes belonging to WHO; the car had been completely crushed. He'd been taken by helicopter to the hospital in Lausanne, and he was phoning her from there. Panicking, Florence wanted to rush to his side, and panicking in turn, he began to play down his injuries. He returned that same evening to Prévessin, driving his own car. The scratches from the brambles didn't look anything like the results of a traffic accident, but Florence was too shaken to notice. He threw himself on their bed in tears. She hugged him to comfort him, gently asking what was going on, why he was suffering. Lately she had had the definite feeling that something was wrong. Still crying, he explained to her that if he'd lost control of the car, it was because he'd had a terrible shock. His supervisor at WHO had just died of a cancer that had been eating away at him for several years. During the summer, the disease had spread rapidly; Jean-Claude had been well aware that all hope was lost, but to see him dead . . . He sobbed all night long. Florence, although deeply moved, was surprised by the strength of his attachment to a superior whom he had never mentioned to her.

Jean-Claude as well must have felt that he needed to offer more of an explanation. At the beginning of autumn, the lymphoma that had been dormant for fifteen years awakened in the form of Hodgkin's disease. Knowing that this would meet with more understanding than a mistress had, he confided in Luc. Listening to him say he was doomed as he sat bloated and miserable, slumped in his armchair, Luc remembered the elated Jean-Claude who had visited him at the construction site. He was wearing the same suit, but it seemed shabby, the collar covered with dandruff. Passion had ravaged him. Now it was attacking his cells. While he did not regret having argued so adamantly for a breakup, Luc felt profound pity for his friend's soul, which he sensed was as sick as his body. Always the optimist, however, he wanted to believe that this trial would bring Jean-Claude back to Florence and lead to a deeper communion between husband and wife. "The two of you talk about it a lot, of course . . ." To his great surprise, Jean-Claude replied that no, they didn't speak about it much. He had informed Florence, dramatizing as little as possible, and they had agreed to behave as if nothing had happened, so as not to cast a pall over the household. She had offered to accompany him to Paris, where he was under the care of Dr. Schwartzenberg (this also astonished Luc: he'd had no idea the world-famous physician was still seeing patients—and that's assuming that he'd ever had office patients at all), but Jean-Claude had refused. It was his cancer, and he would fight it alone, without making demands on anyone else. He was assuming responsibility; she respected his decision.

THE ILLNESS AND TREATMENT EXHAUSTED HIM. HE NO longer went to work every day. Florence got the children up, telling them not to make noise because Papa was tired. After driving them to school, she would have coffee at the home of one of their classmates' mothers, or go to her dance class, her yoga class, perhaps do some shopping. Alone in the house, Jean-Claude spent the day in his damp bed, the comforter drawn up over his head. He had always perspired heavily; now the sheets had to be changed daily. Drenched in unhealthy sweat, he dozed, reading without understanding, stupefied. It was like the year he'd gone to ground in Clairvaux after his failure at the Lycée du Parc: the same gray torpor, shaken by chills.

Despite the declaration of friendship with which they had parted, he had not spoken to Corinne again since the catastrophic trip to Rome. As soon as Florence left the house, he'd hover over the telephone, dialing Corinne's number and hanging up as soon as she lifted the receiver because he was afraid she would be annoyed to hear from him. He was astounded, on the day he dared speak, to find that she was happy he had called. She was going through a very upsetting time: professional difficulties, love affairs with no future. Her loneliness, her children, her disquieting availability were frightening to men, and she had suffered enough from their loutish behavior to welcome hearing from this Dr. Romand who was so sad, so clumsy, but who treated her like a queen. She began to tell him of her disappointments and resentments. He listened to her, comforted her. Deep down beneath the surface, he said, the two of them were much alike. She was his little sister. He returned to Paris in December, and it all began again: the dinners, the evenings out, the presents, and after the New Year, five days of romance in Leningrad.

This trip, which gave rise to wild speculation early in

the investigation, was organized by *Quotidien du Médecin*, a daily newsletter for physicians to which Jean-Claude subscribed. If he had looked around, he could have found dozens of ways to spend a few days in Russia, but it never occurred to him to travel otherwise than with a group of doctors, many of whom knew one another, whereas he knew no one. Corinne was surprised at this, and at how studiously he avoided their traveling companions, cutting short all conversations, keeping aloof. Corinne, on the other hand, would have liked to make some friends. If he felt it beneath him to socialize with them or if, as she thought, he was afraid of any nasty gossip that might reach his wife's ears, why were they traveling with them? No doubt about it, she found him exasperating. After three days, she made the same speech she had in Rome: it was all a mistake, they were better off as friends, big brother and little sister. He burst into tears again and, on the flight home, told her that in any case he had cancer. Soon, he would be dead.

What could one say to that? Corinne was troubled and irritated. He begged her, if she had any affection left for him at all, to telephone him now and then, not at home but at his voice mailbox. Their secret code would be 222 for "I'm thinking of you but there's no need to call back," 221 for "Phone me," 111 for "I love you." (He had the same type of code with Florence, who left the answering service a number from 1 to 9, depending on the urgency of the call.) Anxious to put an end to this scene, Corinne wrote down the numbers, promising to use them. He brought back Russian fur hats with earflaps for his children and nesting dolls for his goddaughter.

HAVING BOTCHED THIS SECOND CHANCE, HE FELL BACK into the same old routine and despair. To explain his presence at home, Florence had told most of their friends about his cancer but had asked them not to tell anyone else, which meant that each of them believed he or she was the only one who knew. Jean-Claude was surrounded by discreet solicitude and strained joviality.

At a dinner in the Ladmirals' home, Rémi, who had gone to see his daughters in Paris, told everyone the latest news about his ex-wife. As unstable as ever, she had wavered between two men to remake her life: a nice guy who was something along the lines of a cardiologist, very big in his field but not much fun, and another man who was definitely more with it, a Parisian dentist who wasn't the type to let her twist him around her little finger. Rémi, without knowing him, would have leaned somewhat toward the first man, figuring that Corinne needed stability and protection; unfortunately she liked her love life sleazy and had chosen the second guy. The expression on Jean-Claude's face when he heard that was truly pitiful, Luc remembers.

As she had promised, she called from time to time and, to show him how much she trusted him, would describe her passionate relationship with the dentist who wouldn't let her twist him around her little finger. He made her suffer but it was stronger than she was, she had him under her skin. Jean-Claude agreed in a doleful voice. He coughed, explaining that the lymphoma was weakening his immune system.

One day, she asked his advice. The office she owned with Rémi in Geneva had been sold. Her share, which she had just received, amounted to 900,000 francs. She was thinking about using it to buy a new office, probably in partnership with someone, but didn't want to rush into anything and, rather than leave the money in her current account, preferred to invest it. The few investments she did have didn't bring in much. Did her big brother have a better idea? Well, of course he did. UOB, Quai des Bergues, Geneva, 18 percent a year. He flew to Paris and went with her to the main branch of her bank, where she withdrew the 900,000 francs in cash; then he took the plane again, as in a scene from a movie, with a small suitcase stuffed with bills. No receipt, no trace. He remembers having said, "If something were to happen to me, all your money would be lost." To which she tenderly replied (this is his version), "If something happened to you, it's not the money I'd be sorry about."

It was the first time he was deceiving not elderly members of his family, anxious only to put their savings to work for their heirs, but a determined young woman who needed her money and was counting on getting it back quickly. She had insisted on that, making sure she could do so whenever she wanted, and he had guaranteed it. As it happened, he was in trouble. The gold mine his mother-in-law had entrusted to him was all gone. During the last two years, his expenses had skyrocketed. In Prévessin, he had adopted the lifestyle of his social set, paying 8,000 francs a month in rent, buying himself a Range Rover for 200,000 francs, replacing it with a BMW for 250,000 francs, and in Paris he'd ruined himself with luxury hotels, expensive dinners, and presents for Corinne. In order to keep going he needed that money, which he deposited in his three Banque Nationale de Paris accounts almost as soon as he got home: the one in Ferney-Voltaire, the one in Lons-le-Saunier, and the one in Geneva. The bank director in Ferney was astonished by these irregular cash deposits but didn't dare question him about his sources of revenue. He had telephoned Jean-Claude several times to propose some investments, some more rational ways of managing his money. Jean-Claude kept putting him off. More than anything else he feared overdrawing his account, which he had once again come perilously close to doing. But he knew that he had only obtained a reprieve and that touching Corinne's money would make catastrophe inevitable.

That threat hung heavily over the final year. Until then the menace had been a constant but vague presence in his life. Every time he walked by someone, or somebody spoke to him, or the phone rang at home, apprehension tied his stomach in knots: the moment had arrived, and his imposture would be brought to light. The danger could come from anywhere, the tiniest event of daily life might set in motion the doomsday scenario that nothing would stop. But now one version of that scenario had become more likely than the others, and no matter how often he remembered what people tell the seriously ill—that it's perfectly possible to have cancer and yet die of a bee sting or the flu—it was that one version he could not stop thinking about. The longer it took the blow to fall, the more surely it would come, leaving him no escape. If Corinne had asked for her money one week after entrusting it to him, he would still have been able to return it to her and search for another way (but which one?) to live as if he had an income even though he didn't. Weeks, months went by; the supposedly invested sum was shrinking. Appalled and bewildered, he didn't even try to make it last, spending it instead in a giddy frenzy. When she asked him for it, what would he do? A few years earlier, he could have tried to replace it by appealing to his usual donors: his parents, his uncle Claude, his in-laws. But he knew, and with good reason, the state of their finances. He'd taken everything from them and spent it all. He had no one left to turn to.

What, then? Tell Corinne that he'd been attacked, that the suitcase of money had been stolen? Confess the truth to her? Part of the truth—that he was in an inextricable financial bind and had dragged her into it with him? The whole truth—seventeen years of lies? Or just collect what was left and take a plane to the ends of the earth? Never come back, vanish. The scandal would erupt within a few hours, but he wouldn't be there to watch the collapse of his family and face the accusations in their eyes. Maybe he could pass for dead, make everyone think he'd committed suicide. There would be no body, but if he abandoned the car, with a farewell note, near a mountain chasm . . . Declared dead, he'd be truly out of reach. The problem was that he would still be alive and that alone, even with money, he wouldn't know what to do with his life. Shedding the skin of Dr. Romand would mean ending up without any skin, more than naked: flayed.

He had known from the beginning that the logical conclusion to his story was suicide. He had often thought about it without ever finding the courage to go through with it, and in a sense, the certainty that he would do it one day let him off for the time being. His life had been spent waiting for the day when he could no longer postpone the inevitable. That day should have arrived a hundred times, and a hundred times, by a miracle or by chance, he had escaped it. Although he had no doubt how all this would end, he was curious to see just how long fate would drag things out.

HE WHO HAD SO OFTEN BEGGED CORINNE TO PHONE HIM and had called his automated answering service over and over to hear her voice again whenever she'd happened to leave him a message—he now preferred to leave his voice mail disconnected. He was playing dead. Afraid of getting Florence, Corinne didn't dare call him at Prévessin. Her best friend kept telling her she was out of her mind to have handed over all her money, without a deposit slip, a proxy agreement, or anything, to a terminal cancer patient. If he died, who would tell her? How did she know he wasn't already dead and buried? The Swiss account was in his name—just how did she think she could get her money back from his widow? Since Corinne was becoming more and more worried, the best friend's husband left urgent messages, in his name, on the answering machine in Prévessin. No reply. It was already the beginning of the summer. Corinne remembered that every July Florence would fill in for the pharmacist in a village in the Jura and that the family would stay with Jean-Claude's parents. She finally tracked them down. If he hadn't called back, it was because he'd been hospitalized for a long time. He'd had radiation therapy and was exhausted. Corinne sympathized with him, then got to the point: she wanted to recover at least some of her money. It wasn't that simple, he objected, there were the penalty periods to consider. "You told me there weren't any, that I could withdraw whatever I wanted, whenever I wanted . . ." Yes, in principle, but only in principle. If she wanted to earn the interest instead of paying any exchange premiums, the account would have to remain untouched until September; in fact it was blocked in any case, and besides, he himself was blocked—ill, bedridden, unable to get to Geneva. All he could do right then was sell his car to help her out. Corinne's temper flared: she was asking him to get her money from the bank, not to sell his car and act as though this were a huge sacrifice. Somehow he managed to calm her down.

HIS VISA CARD RECORDS FOR THAT YEAR SHOW REGULAR purchases of photo-novels and pornographic videos in sex shops as well as massages about twice a month at the Marylin

Center and the Only You Club in Lyon. The employees of these establishments remember a calm, courteous client who didn't say much. He says that when he went for a massage he felt as if he existed, as if he had a body.

When fall arrived, Florence stopped taking the pill. This fact can be interpreted several ways, but according to the testimony of her gynecologist, she was considering having a third child.

AS VICE PRESIDENT OF THE PARENTS' ASSOCIATION AT Saint-Vincent, she was kept busy seeing to the catechism class, organizing the school fair, finding parent volunteers to take student groups skiing or to the pool. Luc Ladmiral was on the administrative board. To distract Jean-Claude from his gloomy thoughts, Luc suggested that his friend join the board as well; at the urging of Florence, he did. For him this was not only a distraction but a way of participating in real life: once a month, he went to a meeting that wasn't fictitious, saw people, spoke with them, and even though he pretended to be a busy man, he would willingly have called for additional meetings.

It so happened that the school principal, a married man and the father of four, took up with one of the teachers, who was also married. The affair became known and was frowned on. Some parents felt that there was no point in sending their children to a Catholic school only to have them exposed to immoral behavior. The administrative board decided to intervene. A meeting was held at Luc's house at the beginning of summer vacation. The idea was to ask the offending principal to resign and the diocesan authorities to replace him with a female teacher who would be above reproach. To avoid any scandal, everything was to be taken care of by the beginning of the fall term, which it was. But those who were there disagree about what was said at the meeting. Luc and the others maintain that their decision was unanimous, that Jean-Claude was in agreement with them. He says that no, he didn't go along with them, that things became heated and they all parted angrily. He insists on the fact that such an attitude was quite unlike him: it would have been much simpler, and more in keeping with his character, to follow his friends' lead.

Since there is no reason to think that the others lied, I suppose that he expressed his disagreement, but so tentatively that not only didn't they remember it afterward, they weren't even aware of it at the time. They were so used to having him approve of everything that they literally did not hear him, and he was so unused to making himself heard that he recalls not the real volume of his disagreement—a mumble, the murmured hint of a reservation—but that of the indignant protest boiling inside him to which he vainly tried to give voice. He heard himself say, with all necessary emphasis, what he would have liked to say, not what the others heard. It's also possible that he didn't say anything at all—only thought about speaking up, dreamed about it, regretted not doing it, and finally imagined that he had. When he got home he told his wife all about the conspiracy against the principal and the chivalrous way in which he had taken the man's side. Florence was virtuous but no prude and did not approve of interfering with people's private lives. She was touched that her husband, so conciliatory by nature, worn down by his illness, preoccupied with matters of infinitely greater importance, should have preferred to put himself out rather than cover up an injustice. And when school began and she found the coup d'état was a fait accompli, the principal demoted to an ordinary teacher and his replacement a woman whose sour bigotry had always exasperated her, Florence mounted a crusade in support of the persecuted man, campaigning among the other mothers with her usual energy and soon rallying many in the parents' association to her side. The school board's decision was contested. The parents' association and the board, which had previously been on good terms with each other, became enemy camps led respectively by Florence Romand and Luc Ladmiral, even though the two were longtime friends. This development poisoned the trimester.

Not content with backing his wife, Jean-Claude poured it on. Picking up his children after school, this peaceful man could be heard loudly declaring that he had fought for human rights in Morocco and was not going to allow them to be trampled in Ferney-Voltaire. Annoyed at being made to look like prigs, supporters of the school board and the new headmistress emphasized that the problem was not so much the immorality of the former principal as the laxity of his management: he wasn't up to the job, that was all. To which Jean-Claude responded that people aren't always up to the job, they can't always do what they want, and that it's better to understand and help than to judge and condemn. Fine principles were one thing, but he preferred to defend naked, fallible man, of whom Saint Paul says that he wishes to do good and cannot keep from doing evil. Was Jean-Claude aware that he was pleading for himself? He was aware, in any case, that he was running a great risk.

For the first time he was drawing attention to himself in their little community. Rumor had it that he was at the root of the whole thing, some saying that he'd switched sides, others that he was a close friend of the disgraced principal; the general impression was that he had played a murky role. Although Luc was angry at his friend, he tried to calm everyone down: Jean-Claude had serious health problems, that's why he was making a mess of things. But the other conspirators on the school board demanded a confrontation, the very idea of which constituted a deadly danger to Jean-Claude. For eighteen years, he had been afraid of this. He had been spared time after time by some miracle and now he was going to be exposed, not through an accident he'd been helpless to avoid but through his own fault, because for the first time in his life he had said what he thought. A neighbor brought news that put the finishing touch to his anguish: it seemed that Serge Bidon, another member of the school board, had talked about bashing his face in.

THE MOST STRIKING TESTIMONY AT THE TRIAL WAS THAT of his uncle, Claude Romand. He walked in, ruddy-complexioned, stocky, squeezed into a suit that seemed about to split open across his powerful shoulders, and when he reached the witness stand, instead of turning to face the court like everyone else, he turned toward his nephew. Arms akimbo, certain that no one would dare say a thing, he looked him up and down. He took his time, perhaps thirty seconds, which is a very long while. Jean-Claude had turned to jelly with fear, and everybody in the room thought the same thing: it wasn't only shame and remorse; despite the distance, the glass panel, the policemen, he was afraid of being hit.

What was written all over him in that moment was his panicky dread of physical violence. He had chosen to live among people in whom the instinct to fight had atrophied, but each time he returned to his village he must have sensed that instinct just below the surface. As an adolescent, he read in Uncle Claude's little pale blue eyes the mocking contempt a man who comfortably inhabits his body and his place on earth feels for the wimp that he was, always buried in a book. Later, behind the clan's admiration for its brilliant scion, he detected a violence that would explode at the first opportunity. Uncle Claude would tease him, thump him affectionately on the back, and like the others, entrust him with money to invest, but only his uncle ever asked about his investment from time to time: if anyone were ever to become suspicious someday, he would be the one. It would take only the merest hint of a misgiving for him to understand right away and corner his nephew. Then he would thrash him. Before filing a complaint, before anything else, he would pound him with his huge fists. He would hurt him.

Serge Bidon, according to those who know him, is the gentlest soul on earth. His threat, if it actually was uttered, was certainly rhetorical. Yet Jean-Claude had been scared to death, no longer daring to go home or to follow his usual routines. His whole body was giving way. Alone in his car, he had sobbed and mumbled, "They want to punch my face in . . . They want to punch my face in . . ."

ON THE LAST SUNDAY IN ADVENT, OUTSIDE THE CHURCH after Mass, Luc left Cécile and their children for a moment to go talk to Florence, who was there with her children but not Jean-Claude. They had exchanged the sign of peace before Communion and read the Gospel in which Jesus says prayer is useless if one is not at peace with one's neighbor, so before Christmas arrived Luc wanted to make peace, to end that ridiculous quarrel between them. "Okay, you disagree with us about demoting that idiot, you have a right to your opinion, people don't have to think the same as their friends about everything, but we're not going to sulk over this for the next hundred years." Florence smiled and they kissed, happy to be friends again. Still, Luc couldn't help adding, if Jean-Claude disagreed with them, he could have said so then and there, they would have talked it over. Florence frowned. That was exactly what he'd done, wasn't it? No, said Luc, that wasn't what he'd done and that was why everyone was upset. Not because he had defended the principal, which, Luc repeated, he had every right to do, but because he had voted with the others to throw him out and only afterward, without consulting anyone, led a campaign against what he himself had approved, making the school board look like a bunch of jerks. While he was talking, going over those grievances he had sincerely decided to set aside, speaking simply because he wished to set the record straight, Luc watched as Florence's face crumpled. "You can swear to me that Jean-Claude voted for dismissal?" Of course he could swear it, and the others could too, but it wasn't important, the hatchet was buried, they'd all celebrate Christmas together. The more he repeated that the incident was closed, the more he realized that for Florence it wasn't closed at all, that the words he considered so harmless were opening an abyss inside her. "He always told me he'd voted against it . . ." Luc didn't even dare tell her anymore that it wasn't serious. He felt that on the contrary it was serious, that something extremely serious and incomprehensible to him was at stake in that moment. He seemed to see Florence imploding right there in front of him at the church door, and he felt helpless. She touched the children nervously, adjusted Antoine's hood, held on to Caroline's hand as her daughter tugged impatiently; her fingers had begun moving around like drunken wasps, and her lips, now bloodless, kept saying softly, "So he lied to me. He lied to me."

THE NEXT DAY WHEN SCHOOL LET OUT SHE CHATTED briefly with a lady whose husband also worked at WHO. The woman was planning on taking her daughter to the Christmas tree party for employees' children and wanted to know if Antoine and Caroline would be there. At these words Florence turned pale and murmured, "This time, I really should get annoyed with my husband."

At the trial, when the lawyers were trying to interpret this evidence, Jean-Claude said that Florence had known for years about the children's party for WHO personnel. They had talked about it several times, he refusing to let the children go because he didn't like to take advantage of such perks, she regretting that his overly strict principles were depriving them of a pleasant occasion. The lady's question could have revived Florence's irritation but not produced the effect of a revelation. Besides, he pointed out, if she'd had the slightest doubt, all she had to do was pick up the phone and call WHO.

"And how do you know she didn't?" asked the judge.

. . .

JUST BEFORE CHRISTMAS VACATION THE PRESIDENT OF THE
school board wanted to talk to Jean-Claude, still on the
subject of the demoted principal. The president did not
know Jean-Claude well enough to be aware that one didn't
call him at his office, and since he himself worked in Geneva
for an international organization, he had his secretary look
up his number in the WHO directory. And then in the
international organizations' pension fund database. Puzzled
at not finding him anywhere, he figured there must be some
explanation, and as it wasn't very important, he didn't think
about it again until one day after the vacation when he ran
into Florence on the main street of Ferney and told her about
it. His tone wasn't that of a man who had suspicions but
that of someone who was curious to find out the real story
behind an odd mystery, and Florence reacted equally mildly.
It was strange, yes, there was obviously a reason, and she'd
speak to her husband about it. Florence and the man did
not see each other again, one week later she was dead, and
no one will ever know if she brought it up with Jean-Claude.
He says she didn't.

ALTHOUGH HE WAS UNSURE WHERE THE FIRST BLOW
would come from, he knew that the hounds were closing in.
His various bank accounts would soon be overdrawn, and he
had no means of replenishing them. People were talking
about him, and talking about coming after him. Someone

was going around Ferney threatening to smash his face in. Hands were flipping through directories. The look in Florence's eyes had changed. He was scared. He telephoned Corinne. She was depressed: she had just broken up with the dentist who didn't let her twist him around her little finger. A few months earlier, this would have given him new hope. Now it didn't make much difference, but he acted like a king in a chess game who, menaced on all sides, has only a single square left: objectively, the game is lost, he should give up—but he moves to that square anyway, if only to see how his adversary will set up the trap. That same day, he flew to Paris and took Corinne to dinner at the Restaurant Michel Rostang, where he gave her a picture frame of burled elm wood and a leather correspondence case from Lancel's that cost 2,120 francs. For two hours, in the circle of soft light that sealed off their table, he felt safe. He played the role of Dr. Romand, thinking all the while that it was for the last time but that nothing mattered anymore, for soon he would be dead. At the end of the dinner, Corinne told him that she had made up her mind and she wanted her money back. Instead of trying to wriggle out of it, he opened his datebook to set up a meeting when he would hand over the funds. Turning the pages, he had an idea: he had agreed to have dinner at the beginning of the new year with his friend Bernard Kouchner. Would Corinne like to join them? Of course Corinne would like that. Preferably on a Saturday, the ninth or sixteenth of January—Kouchner had left it up to him. The ninth, then, Corinne decided, that was earlier. Jean-Claude would have preferred the sixteenth, which left more time, but he said nothing. The die was cast. Before the ninth of January, he would be dead. On the flight home, he continued to study his datebook, like a businessman with much on his mind. Christmas wasn't a good day, that would be too cruel for the children. Caroline was going to play Mary and Antoine one of the shepherds in the Nativity scene at the church. So, right after New Year's?

HE WENT TO GET HIS PARENTS IN CLAIRVAUX SO THEY could spend Christmas with them. In the trunk of his car, under the Christmas tree, he brought back a box of papers taken from his childhood bedroom: old letters, memo pads, an exercise book bound in velvet in which, he asserted, Florence had written love poems for him when they'd become engaged. He burned everything out in the back of the garden, with other cardboard boxes from the attic containing his personal notebooks. He says that over the years, without really bothering to hide them, he had filled dozens of notebooks with more or less autobiographical texts that appeared to be fiction (to fool Florence if she should happen across them) yet followed reality closely enough to constitute a confession. But she never found them, or wasn't curious enough to open them, or never spoke to him about them— or else, a last hypothesis, these notebooks did not exist.

He also says that he wanted to leave a message for Florence to find after his death and that between Christmas and New Year's he made endless rough drafts. Of letters but also of cassettes he would tape, alone in his car, on a small tape recorder: "Forgive me, I don't deserve to live, I lied to you but my love for you and the children was not a lie." He couldn't do it. "Every time I began, I'd put myself in her place as she read or listened to that and . . ."

He chokes, and hangs his head.

That last week, he felt tired, heavy. He would doze off on the sofa, in his car, any time at all. There was a ringing in his ears as if he'd been to the bottom of the ocean. His brain hurt—he would have liked to take it out of his skull and put it through the wash. After coming back from Strasbourg, where they had celebrated New Year's Eve at the home of friends who were doctors, Florence did some laundry and he stayed in the bathroom, watching through the window in the washing machine's door as the clothes tumbled limply in the scalding water. Impregnated with his unhealthy perspiration, there were his shirts and underwear mixed in with Florence's and the children's, Antoine's and Caroline's T-shirts, their pajamas decorated with tiny cartoon animals, their little socks that were so hard to tell apart when you were putting them away. The whole family's jumbled clothing, their breaths mingling peacefully beneath the snug roof that sheltered them from the winter's night . . . It should have been good to come home together on a New Year's Day, one big happy family in the Renault Espace that purred over the snowy road; to arrive late, carry the sleeping children up to their room, and help them undress (Hop! Into bed!); to hunt through the bags for the stuffed rabbit Antoine liked to snuggle with, and to be relieved because they hadn't forgotten it in Strasbourg after all; to listen to Florence joking about it as she wiped off her makeup (That was a close call—you'd have had to drive all the way back!); to be the last one up, standing in the bathroom that separated the room where the children were sleeping from the one where Florence was waiting for him beneath the comforter. Her head turned away so as not to have the light in her eyes, she would hold his hand while he read. It should have been warm and cozy, that family life. They thought it was warm and cozy. But he knew that it was rotten at the core, that not one moment, not one gesture, not even their slumbers had escaped this rot that had grown within him, gradually eating everything away from inside without showing anything on the outside, and now it was all that was left, nothing but the rot that would burst through the shell into broad daylight. They would find themselves naked, defenseless, out in the cold and the horror, and that would be the only reality. Even if they didn't know it, it was already the only reality. He pushed open the door, tiptoed over to the children. They were asleep. He watched them sleeping. He couldn't do that to them. They couldn't know that it was he, their papa, who had done that to them.

THEY SPENT SUNDAY AT THE WOOD GROUSE, THE CHALET they often went to on the mountain pass of La Faucille. An excellent skier, Florence had taught the children. Under her supervision, they could go almost everywhere. He stayed inside, reading at a table in the restaurant, where they joined him for lunch. Antoine proudly told how he'd been on a red trail and at one point, on a difficult turn, he'd almost fallen but then hadn't. The children were allowed to order huge plates of French fries and ketchup, which was one of their reasons for adoring the Wood Grouse. In the car, on the way there, they'd chant like a litany: "Can we have fries? Can we have fries?" Florence would say yes and they'd up the ante: "Can we have seconds? Can we have two plates each? Three plates each?"

MONDAY MORNING HIS MOTHER PHONED HIM, QUITE upset. She had just received a bank statement indicating an overdraft of forty thousand francs. It was the first time that had happened; she hadn't dared mention it to her husband, it would have worried him too much. Jean-Claude said he'd take care of things, transfer funds from another account, and she hung up reassured, as she always was after speaking with her son. (The letter informing her that their account was frozen arrived the following week.)

Bringing along his copy of Bernard Kouchner's book *The Misfortune of Others*, personally dedicated during a signing session at a bookstore in Geneva ("To Jean-Claude, my good friend and colleague at WHO—Bernard"), he'd driven to the airport at Cointrin, bought a bottle of perfume, and taken the 12:15 flight to Paris. In the cabin, where he recognized the minister of employment, Jacques Barrot, among the passengers, he wrote a short letter to Corinne (". . . I must make some decisions this week. I'm happy to be spending Saturday evening with you. It will be a farewell, perhaps, or a new reprieve: you will decide") and searched through Kouchner's book for a passage that had deeply affected him, about the suicide of one of the author's oldest friends. The friend was an anesthesiologist. Even as he was swallowing, in careful order, the ingredients of a deadly and irreversible cocktail, he had telephoned a woman he loved to keep her informed, minute by minute, of the progress of his agony. She had only one phone line and knew that if she hung up to call for help he would immediately give himself a lethal injection. She had to listen to a live report of his death.

Hoping that Corinne would read and understand, he slipped his letter in at that page and left book and perfume at her office. He doesn't remember anything else about his visit to Paris, and what with taxi rides, he hardly had time to do anything else, because he flew back on the 4:30 plane to keep an appointment at his garage in Ferney. Since selling the BMW, he had rented a Renault 21, followed by the Espace, which he felt—these are his words—"wasn't that exciting anymore." He wanted to get another four-door sedan. After some hesitation, he chose a metallic green BMW equipped with numerous options, and he drove it home.

HE DID NOT GO TO WORK ON TUESDAY. FLORENCE AND HE ran errands in Ferney. She insisted that he buy a new suit; he let himself be tempted by a parka for thirty-two hundred francs. The saleswoman thought they seemed a couple who were at leisure, well-off, and getting along fine. They went to Saint-Vincent to pick up the children and Sophie Ladmiral, who was to sleep over at their house. Florence took them all home for their after-school snack, dropping Jean-Claude off at the Pharmacie Cottin. He had spent the morning studying *Final Exit* and the Vidal pharmacological dictionary, rejecting drugs that caused instantaneous death (cyanide salts, anything having an effect similar to that of curare) in favor of barbiturates with a rapid serum peak, which were recommended in conjunction with an antiemetic, for a comfortable lapse into unconsciousness. He needed these drugs, he explained to Cottin, for his research on cell cultures. Although he might reasonably have wondered why a researcher would come to a pharmacy for substances that should normally have been provided by his laboratory, Cottin showed no surprise. As professionals, they examined his microfiches together and selected two barbiturates, to which, just to be safe, Cottin proposed adding a solution with a phenobarbital basis that he would make up himself. Everything would be ready by Friday, would that do? It would do.

That evening, with his goddaughter on his lap, Romand read a story to the three children. Since they had run around a lot the previous day and didn't have school Wednesday morning, the kids got up late and played in pajamas until lunchtime. He left for Lyon. At 2:08 he obtained a thousand francs from the Banque Nationale de Paris ATM on the Place Bellecour, and another thousand francs at 2:45. Between the two withdrawals, he says, he gave a five-hundred-franc bill to a homeless person. Then, in a gun shop, he bought a stun wand, two tear gas canisters, a box of cartridges, and a silencer for a .22 caliber rifle.

"So," the judge pointed out, "you weren't thinking only of killing yourself. You were living with your wife and children while you were planning to kill them."

"That idea did surface . . . but it was immediately masked by other false plans, other false ideas. It was as though the idea didn't exist . . . I pretended . . . I told myself I was doing something else, that it was for a different reason, and at the same time . . . at the same time I was buying the bullets that would pierce my children's hearts."

He sobbed.

· · ·

HE HAD HIS PURCHASES GIFT-WRAPPED, TELLING HIMSELF that the self-defense weapons were for Corinne, who was afraid when she came home in the evening, and that the cartridges and silencer were for his father, who had not been able to use his rifle for years because he was almost blind.

While he was buying these things, Florence was serving tea to two friends whose children also went to Saint-Vincent. She did not confide in them, but at some point that her guests do not recall precisely she showed them the framed photo of a little boy of six or seven on the mantelpiece. "Look how cute he is," she said. "Look at those eyes. There can't be anything bad behind those eyes." Somewhat disconcerted, the two women looked at the photo and agreed that Jean-Claude really had been very cute. Florence changed the subject.

ON THURSDAY, THE DAY EVERYONE THOUGHT HE TAUGHT a class in Dijon, he always left early so he could swing by Clairvaux to see his parents. Their doctor, who ran into him in front of their house, helped him unload a case of mineral water he'd bought for them. Romand looked through some old toxicology notes up in his room and reassured his mother about their financial situation. The public prosecutor wondered if the true reason for his visit wasn't to get his father's rifle, for which he had bought ammunition and a silencer the day before, but Romand says no: he had brought it back with him to Prévessin the previous summer to shoot targets in his backyard (no testimony mentions this pastime). On the way home, he telephoned Corinne and made a point of reminding her about the dinner at Kouchner's on Saturday. Then he went by the Ladmirals' to return a pair of slippers Sophie had left at his house. He says that he hoped to see Luc and tell him the truth, that he considered this visit his last chance, and that unfortunately he found a rather frazzled Cécile: one of their friends had just had a baby, and Cécile had to take care of the woman's children. He knew that at five in the afternoon Luc would never be at home but at his office. He did not go there. That evening, as he did every evening, he called his parents to wish them good night.

ON FRIDAY HE DROVE THE CHILDREN TO SCHOOL, BOUGHT a newspaper and croissants, and waited with a neighbor (who found him cheerful) for the pharmacy to open. He picked up his bottles of barbiturates and a pack of chewing gum that was supposed to be good for the teeth, then joined Florence at the one florist's shop in Ferney. They sent the new mother an azalea along with a note they both signed. While she dashed off to her class in china painting, he went to the Continent supermarket, where he bought two jerry cans as well as an object that cost, according to the receipt, forty francs. (The prosecution established that for this price one could purchase a rolling pin. Jean-Claude thinks he remembers a metal bar intended to replace a broken ladder rung, but neither that bar not the broken ladder has been found.) He filled the jerry cans with gas at the Continent's service station. Coming home for lunch, he found a guest, a pleasant young blonde who was Caroline's teacher. They talked about a skit she wanted her students to put on, for which she needed large quantities of bandages for mummy costumes. Always obliging, he said he could get as much gauze as he wanted from the hospital in Geneva and promised to see to it. Since the children were invited the next day to a birthday party for their friend Nina, the daughter of an African diplomat, they had to buy a present. After school the whole family went to pick out a box of Legos in a shopping center in Switzerland. They had supper in the cafeteria and came home early. Antoine and Caroline, in pajamas, made drawings to go with the gift. After the children had gone to bed, Florence had a long phone conversation with her mother, who was hurt at not having been invited to a cousin's wedding. She complained bitterly about being a widow, about growing old, about being neglected by her children. Her unhappiness affected Florence, who began crying after she hung up. Jean-Claude joined her on the sofa. That is the last image he has. He is sitting next to her, he has taken her in his arms, he is trying to comfort her.

"I don't remember," he says, "her last words."

• • •

AT THE AUTOPSY, FLORENCE'S BLOOD ALCOHOL LEVEL WAS found to be .20, which suggests, if she had a full night's rest, that she went to sleep in a state close to intoxication. And she never drank—at most she had a glass of wine on special occasions. One imagines a quarrel beginning with these words: "I know that you lie to me." He's evasive, she insists: Why tell her that he'd voted against dismissing the principal? Why isn't he listed in the WHO directory? The discussion becomes heated, she has a drink to calm down, then another, and a third. Thanks to the alcohol, which she isn't used to, she winds up falling asleep. He stays awake, spends the night wondering how to get himself out of this situation, and at dawn smashes her skull in.

When this scenario is proposed to him, he replies: "If we'd had a fight, why would I hide it? I wouldn't feel less guilty but it would be an explanation . . . It would perhaps be more acceptable . . . I can't say for certain that it didn't happen, but I don't remember it. I remember the other murder scenes, which are just as horrible, but not that one. I am unable to say what happened between the time when I was consoling Florence on the sofa and the moment I woke up holding the rolling pin stained with blood."

According to the prosecution, he bought it at the supermarket the day before; he says it was lying around the children's bedroom, where they'd been using it to roll out

EMMANUEL CARRÈRE

modeling clay. After he'd used it in turn, he washed it in the bathroom, carefully enough that no trace of blood could be seen with the naked eye, then put it away.

THE TELEPHONE RANG. HE ANSWERED IT IN THE BATH-room. It was a friend, a psychologist in Prévessin, who wanted to know if Florence would be helping her take charge of the catechism Mass that Saturday evening. He told her no, prob-ably not, because they were planning on spending the night with his parents in the Jura. He apologized for speaking softly: the children were asleep and Florence too. He offered to go get her if it was important but the woman said not to bother—she'd manage the Mass on her own.

The phone call had awakened the children, who piled into the bathroom. They were always quicker to bounce out of bed on days when they didn't have school. He told them as well that Mama was still sleeping, and the three of them went downstairs to the living room. He put a tape of *The Three Little Pigs* in the VCR, fixed bowls of Cocoa Puffs with milk. With him in the middle, they settled themselves on the sofa to watch the cartoon while they ate their cereal.

"AFTER I KILLED FLORENCE, I KNEW THAT I WAS ALSO going to kill Antoine and Caroline and that those moments in front of the television were the last that we would spend together. I cuddled with them. I must have said sweet things to them, like 'I love you.' I did that a lot, and they'd often

138

draw pictures for me. Even Antoine, who didn't know how to write well yet, could write 'I love you.'"

A very long silence. The judge, in a changed voice, suggested a five-minute recess, but he shook his head and we heard him swallow before he went on.

"We stayed like that for perhaps an hour . . . Caroline saw that I was cold, she wanted to go upstairs to get my bathrobe . . . I said that I thought *they* seemed rather hot, that perhaps they had a fever and I was going to take their temperature. Caroline went upstairs with me, I had her lie down on her bed . . . I went to get the rifle . . ."

THE EPISODE OF THE DOG BEGAN AGAIN. HE STARTED shaking, seemed on the verge of collapse. He threw himself on the floor. You couldn't see him anymore—court officers were bending over him. In a little boy's shrill voice he moaned, "My papa! My papa!" A woman ran from the courtroom audience toward the witness stand and pounded on the glass panel, saying, "Jean-Claude! Jean-Claude!" in a pleading voice, like a mother. No one had the heart to restrain her.

"WHAT DID YOU SAY TO CAROLINE?" ASKED THE JUDGE after a half-hour recess.

"I don't know anymore . . . She'd lain down on her stomach . . . That's when I shot her."

"Go on . . ."

"I already had to tell the examining magistrate, many times, but now . . . now, *they* are here." He sobbed. "I shot Caroline the first time . . . She had a pillow over her head . . . I must have been pretending it was a game." Here he moaned, his eyes closed. "I pulled the trigger . . . I put the rifle somewhere in the room . . . I called Antoine . . . and I did it again."

"Perhaps I should help you a bit, because the jury needs details and you're not being specific enough."

"Caroline, when she was born, it was the most wonderful day of my life . . . She was beautiful"—he moaned—"in my arms . . . for her first bath." A spasm shook his body. "I'm the one who killed her . . . I'm the one who killed her."

The policemen, appalled, held him gently by the arms.

"Don't you think Antoine could have heard the gunshots? Had you attached the silencer? Did you call him upstairs on the same pretext? To take his temperature? He didn't find that strange?"

"I don't have an image of that precise moment. It was still them, but it couldn't be Caroline . . . it couldn't be Antoine . . ."

"Didn't he go over to Caroline's bed? You'd covered her with her comforter so he wouldn't suspect anything . . ."

He sobbed again.

"You said during the preliminary investigation that you'd tried to give Antoine some phenobarbital diluted in a glass of water and that he refused, saying that it didn't taste good."

"That was more like a deduction . . . I don't have any image of Antoine saying it didn't taste good."

"No other explanation?"

"Maybe I wanted him to be already asleep."

The prosecutor spoke up. Afterward, he said, Romand went out to buy the local paper and a sports daily, *L'Equipe*, and the newspaper vendor thought he looked completely normal.

"Were you trying to behave as if nothing had happened, as if life were going on as usual?"

"I couldn't have bought *L'Equipe*. I never read it."

"Neighbors saw you cross the street to check your mailbox."

"Did I do it to deny reality, to pretend?"

"Why did you wrap up the rifle and carefully put it in the car before you left for Clairvaux?"

"In reality, to kill them, of course, but I must have told myself that it was to return it to my father."

BECAUSE HIS PARENTS' LABRADOR ALWAYS DIRTIED HIS clothes with an exuberant welcome, he put on jeans and an old jacket but hung the suit he would wear for the dinner in Fontainebleau on the clothes hook in the car. He put a spare shirt and his shaving kit in an overnight bag.

He doesn't remember the drive.

He remembers parking in front of the statue of the Virgin that his father maintained and decorated with flowers every week. He can still see him opening the front door. After that, there are no more images until his death.

We know the three of them had lunch together. Dishes were still on the table when Uncle Claude entered the house two days later, and the autopsy revealed that the stomachs of Aimé and Anne-Marie were full. Did Jean-Claude eat anything? Did his mother urge him to have something? What did they talk about?

He had made his children go upstairs, each in turn, and he did the same thing with his parents. First his father, whom he lured into his former bedroom with the excuse of examining a malodorous air vent the old man had complained about. Unless Jean-Claude took the rifle to his room as soon as he arrived, he must have been carrying it when he went up with his father. Since the gun rack wasn't upstairs, he might have said that he was going to shoot at targets in the garden from the window; it's more likely that he said nothing at all. Why would Aimé Romand have worried about seeing his son carrying the rifle they'd gone to buy together on the boy's sixteenth birthday? The old man, who couldn't bend over because of back trouble, must have knelt down to point out the defective vent, which was set into the baseboard. That was when he received two bullets in the back. He fell forward. His son covered him with a wine-colored corduroy bedspread that had been in the room since Jean-Claude's childhood.

Then he went to get his mother. She hadn't heard the gunshots, fired with a silencer. He had her go into the sitting room, which they never used. She was the only one who was shot from the front. He must have tried, by showing her something, to make her turn around. Did she turn back sooner than expected to see her son aiming the rifle at her? Did she say, "Jean-Claude, what's the matter?" or "What's the matter with you?" as he stated during one of the interrogations, only to claim later that he didn't remember that anymore and knew of it only through the case file? With that same uncertainty, trying like the rest of us to reconstruct the scene, he says that his mother lost her false teeth when she fell and that he put them back in for her before covering her with a green bedspread.

The dog, which had come upstairs with his mother, ran from one body to the other in confusion, whining softly. "I thought that Caroline should have him with her," he says. "She adored him." Romand adored him too, to the point of always carrying his picture in his wallet. After shooting him, he covered him with a blue eiderdown.

He went back downstairs with the rifle, which he cleaned with cold water—since blood washes off better with cold water—and then put away in the gun rack. He changed from his jeans and old jacket to his suit but kept on the same shirt: he was sweating, so it was better to change it when he got to Paris. He telephoned Corinne, and they agreed to meet at the Eglise d'Auteuil, where she would be accompanying her daughters to the Brownies' Mass. He carefully closed up the house and drove off at around two o'clock.

"When I left Clairvaux, I did the same thing I always did: I looked back at the front door and the house. I always did that because my parents were old and sick and I'd tell myself that it could be the last time I would see them."

HAVING TOLD CORINNE HE WOULD DO HIS BEST TO ATTEND Mass with her and her daughters, he spent the trip checking his watch and the remaining distance to Paris. Before he reached the expressway, while he was on a bumpy secondary road in Lons-le-Saunier, he remembers driving a little carelessly, something he never did. It was Saturday evening; at the tollbooth, where the line advanced slowly, he grew impatient, and his irritation increased on the beltway around Paris. Although he'd thought it would take him only fifteen minutes to get from the Porte d'Orléans exit to the Porte d'Auteuil, it took him forty-five. The Mass was not celebrated in the nave of the church but in a downstairs chapel whose entrance he had trouble finding. Arriving late, he stayed in the back and did not go forward for Communion; he's certain of that, because if he had taken Communion he would have gone to sit next to Corinne afterward. Instead of which, as the first one to leave, he waited for them outside.

He kissed the two little girls, whom he hadn't seen in over a year, and the four of them went up to Corinne's apartment. He chatted with the baby-sitter. While their mother changed and freshened her makeup, Léa and Chloé showed him the presents they'd received for Christmas. When Corinne reappeared, she was wearing a pink suit and the ring he had given her as a peace offering after his first declaration of love. On the beltway, which he now took in the opposite direction, she asked for her money. He apologized for not having had the time to go to Geneva, but said he would go Monday morning without fail, then take the 12:15 flight, so she would have everything by early that afternoon. She was a little annoyed, but her excitement over the glittering dinner party that awaited them soon returned. They left the expressway at Fontainebleau, and from then on she gave him directions from a map on which he had marked with a cross, at random, the location of Kouchner's house. They were looking for "a little road on the left." The map wasn't very detailed, which helped explain at first why they were having trouble getting their bearings. After driving around in the forest for an hour, he stopped to look in the trunk for a piece of paper on which he'd written Kouchner's phone number, but he didn't find it. When Corinne began to worry about their being late, he reassured her: other guests who were also researchers were coming from Geneva and wouldn't arrive before 10:30. To distract her, he began to talk about his coming transfer to Paris, the directorship of INSERM he had finally accepted, and his company apartment in Saint-Germain-des-Prés. He described the floor plan to her, saying specifically that he expected to live there alone. The previous evening, he and Florence had had a long discussion about the directions their lives were taking, and they had agreed that it was better that way. The hardest part, he sighed, would be not seeing the children every day. They were to spend the night at their grandmother's in Annecy after going to a birthday party that afternoon . . . Corinne was getting impatient. He says that at this point all he was thinking about was gaining some time and finding a plausible reason for backing out of the dinner. At around 10:30, he stopped again at a picnic area, determined to tear the trunk apart until he found Kouchner's number. He spent a few minutes rummaging through old boxes containing books and magazines as well as a cassette on which he'd videotaped moments from their trip to Leningrad two years earlier. One glance at Corinne, who was growing more and more upset in the front passenger seat, convinced him that this was not the moment to evoke those tender memories. He returned, sheepishly saying that he hadn't found the paper. He had, however, found a necklace he'd been looking forward to giving her. Corinne shrugged: so what. But he insisted and finally persuaded her to wear it, at least for the evening. She got out of the car so that he could put it on her the way he'd always done with the jewelry he gave her, making her close her eyes.

First she felt, on her face and neck, the burning foam of the tear gas spray. She half opened her eyes but closed them immediately because they stung even more, and as he continued to spray her she began to struggle, fighting with all her strength, so that he felt as though she were the aggressor. They rolled the entire length of the car. A hard cylindrical bar held against Corinne's stomach was giving her electric shocks: it was the stun wand he had planned to give her. Convinced she was going to die, she screamed, "I don't want to! Don't kill me! Think of Léa and Chloé!" and opened her eyes.

Looking into his saved her life. All of a sudden, it was over.

He was standing in front of her, speechless, distraught, holding out his hands—no longer as a murderer would but like a man trying to calm someone who is having hysterics.

"But Corinne," he kept saying softly, "but Corinne . . . calm down . . ."

He had her sit in the car, where the two of them collected themselves as though they'd both just fought off an attack from someone else. They wiped their faces with paper towels and mineral water. He must have managed to spray himself, because his skin and eyes were irritated, too. After a moment, she asked if they were still going to Kouchner's for dinner; they decided not to. He started the car, left the picnic area, and drove slowly back the way they had come. What had just happened seemed as incomprehensible to him as to her, and in her stunned confusion she almost let herself be convinced that she was the one who had started it all. But she was able to resist that idea. She patiently explained to him that no, *he* was the one. She told him how everything had happened. He listened, shaking his head in dismay.

At the first village, he went to call Kouchner to say they weren't coming, and she wasn't even surprised that he now had the phone number. She stayed in the car; he had—automatically or not—put the ignition key in his pocket before going to the phone booth. She watched him, beneath the neon lighting, talking or pretending to talk. The judge wanted to know if he'd dialed a number; he doesn't remember but he thinks he might have called his home in Prévessin and listened to the recording on his answering machine.

When he returned, she asked him if he'd picked up the necklace and he replied no, but it wasn't important—he'd kept the receipt, the insurance company would reimburse him. She realized that at no time had she seen this necklace, whereas she had seen, fallen among the dead leaves by the side of the car, a flexible plastic cord that seemed quite appropriate for strangling someone. During the entire trip back, which took more than two hours because he was driving very slowly, she was afraid his murderous rage would flare up again. Now it was her turn to distract him. She spoke to him both as a devoted friend and as a professional psychologist. He blamed everything on his illness. This cancer wasn't satisfied with killing him, it was driving him mad. Often, lately, he'd had moments of absence, blank spaces he couldn't recall. He wept. She nodded with a competent and understanding air when in reality she was scared stiff. He absolutely had to see someone, she said. Someone? A psychiatrist? Yes, or a psychotherapist; she could recommend some very good people to him. Or else he could ask Kouchner—a close friend, he'd often told her, a deeply sensitive and understanding man; it would be a good idea to talk it all over with him. She even offered to call Kouchner herself to tell him, without any dramatizing, exactly what had happened. Yes, he agreed, that was a good idea. This affectionate plan by Kouchner and Corinne to save him from his demons moved him to tears. He began crying again, and she as well. They were both crying when he dropped her off in front of her place at around one in the morning. He made her promise not to say a word to anyone, and she made him promise to return her money, all her money, by Monday. Five minutes later, he called her from a booth where he could see the still-lighted windows of her apartment. "Promise me," he said, "not to believe it was premeditated. If I'd wanted to kill you, I'd have done it in your apartment, and I'd have killed your girls, too."

THE SUN WAS UP WHEN HE ARRIVED IN PRÉVESSIN. HE'D taken a nap at a rest stop near Dijon because fatigue was making him wander over the white line and he was afraid of having an accident. He parked in front of the house, its shutters still closed as he had left them. It felt good to be inside. The living room was a touch untidy but in a homey-looking way, exactly as they would have found it returning from a weekend in Clairvaux or up at La Faucille: the drawings the children had made for Nina's birthday were lying on the table along with the crowns from the Twelfth Night cake. The Christmas tree had lost most of its needles, but they protested whenever he talked about throwing it out, insisting he wait; it was a little ritual they'd managed to stretch into mid-February last year. As he always did when he came home, he turned the page on the desk calendar and checked the message machine. Either there weren't any new messages or he erased them. He dozed a moment on the couch.

At around 11:00 A.M., he became frightened that friends, seeing the car outside, might decide to drop in for a visit, so he went out again to leave it in the parking lot at the Prévessin shopping center. That is doubtless when he wrote, on the back of an envelope, the note that so intrigued the investigators. Returning home, he ran into Cottin, and they greeted each other. The pharmacist asked him whether he'd taken up jogging. Going for a little walk, he replied.

Great, have a nice Sunday.

WE HAVE TWO SOURCES OF INFORMATION TO RECON-struct the rest of his day.

The first is a videocassette he popped into the VCR in place of *The Three Little Pigs*. For three hours, he taped bits

and pieces of programs broadcast on the ten stations he
received via satellite: variety shows and sports, the usual
Sunday afternoon fare, but chopped up by a frantic zapping—one second on one channel, two seconds on another.
It all forms a grim, unwatchable chaos that the investigators forced themselves to watch anyway. They even went so
far as to identify each microsequence and establish the exact
time of its taping by viewing the programs on the various
broadcasting channels. It was thus determined that he
stayed on the couch playing with the remote control
between 1:00 and 4:00 P.M. but also that he began when
the cassette was in midtape. When he reached the end, he
took care to rewind it and erase the entire first part with his
zapping, which tends to indicate that he wanted to erase
something previously taped. Since he says he doesn't
remember this at all, we are reduced to conjectures. The
most likely is that the videotape held images of Florence
and the children: holidays, birthdays, family happiness.
However, during questioning about his purchases in sex
shops and the pornographic videos he claims to have
watched sometimes with his wife, he added that he even
filmed their lovemaking with his video camera. No trace
remains of the cassette, if it ever existed, and the judge
wondered if it wasn't that tape he had so methodically
destroyed on the last day. He says no, he doesn't think so.

In addition, the detailed records of France Télécom show
that between 4:13 and 6:49 he called Corinne's number nine

times. The length of these calls, brief and identical, confirms that nine times he simply listened to the message on her answering machine. The tenth time, she picked up and they spoke for thirteen minutes. Their statements about this conversation support each other. She had spent a ghastly day, said she was extremely shocked, still in pain from her burns, and he sympathized, understood, apologized, spoke of his own depressed state. In light of that state and his illness, she was willing not to inform the police—though any normal person would, she emphasized—but he had to see someone urgently, had to talk to Kouchner or whomever he wanted about what had happened, and above all he had to keep his promise to go the very next morning to get her money from the bank. He swore he would be there when it opened.

He hadn't gone upstairs since his return, but he knew what he would see there. He had carefully pulled up the comforters, but he knew what was under them. At nightfall, he understood that the hour of death, so long postponed, had arrived. He says he began his preparations right away, but he is mistaken: he delayed some more. It was not before midnight and probably, according to the experts, at around three in the morning that he poured the contents of the jerry cans purchased and filled with gas at the Continent, first around the attic, then on the children, on Florence, and in the stairwell. Later he undressed, put on pajamas. Shortly

before 4:00 A.M., he started fires—first in the attic, next in
the stairwell, lastly in the children's room—and then
entered his own bedroom. A surer method would have been
to take the barbiturates in advance, but he must have forgotten or lost them because he wound up using a bottle of
Nembutal he'd kept for ten years in the back of the medicine
chest. At the time he'd thought to use it to ease the agony
of one of his dogs, but that hadn't proved necessary. Later
he had considered throwing it out because the expiration
date had long since passed. He must have thought that it
would still do the trick, and while street cleaners who had
spied the fire on the roof during their morning round were
beginning to pound on the door downstairs, he swallowed
some twenty capsules. The electricity blew; smoke began to
pour into the room. He shoved some clothing against the
bottom of the door to make it airtight, then tried to lie
down next to Florence, who seemed, under the comforter,
to be sleeping. But he couldn't see well, his eyes were sting-
ing, he hadn't set their room alight yet, and the firemen,
whose siren he claims not to have heard, were already there.
No longer able to breathe, he dragged himself to the window
and opened it. The firemen heard the shutters slam apart.
They raised their ladder to rescue him. He lost consciousness.

After coming out of his coma, he began by denying everything. A man dressed in black, a burglar, had shot the children and set the house on fire. Jean-Claude had been paralyzed, helpless, watching it all unfold before his eyes like a nightmare. When the examining magistrate accused him of the massacre at Clairvaux, he became indignant: "You don't kill your father and mother, it's God's second commandment!" When the magistrate proved that Jean-Claude wasn't a researcher at WHO, he said he worked as a scientific consultant for a company called South Arab United something, Quai des Bergues, Geneva. They checked; there was no South Arab United something, Quai des Bergues in Geneva, so he backpedaled and immediately concocted a different story. During seven hours of interrogation, he disputed every piece of evidence. Finally, from exhaustion, or because his lawyer convinced him that this absurd defense would harm him later on, he confessed.

PSYCHIATRISTS WERE ASSIGNED TO EXAMINE HIM. THEY were struck by the precision of his statements and his constant concern with making a favorable impression. He was obviously underestimating the difficulty of giving a favorable impression when one has just murdered one's family after having deceived and defrauded one's relatives for eighteen long years. He was surely also having trouble separating himself from the character he had played all those years, because in an effort to win people over, he still used the same techniques that had worked for Dr. Romand: composure, a dignified gravity, an almost obsequious attention to the expectations of his interlocutor. Such control betrayed serious confusion, because in his normal state, Dr. Romand was intelligent enough to understand that prostration, incoherence, or the cries of a mortally wounded animal would have pleaded more in his favor, given the circumstances, than that worldly professional attitude. Thinking it would help, he didn't realize he was stunning the psychiatrists by giving them a perfectly articulated narrative of his imposture, by speaking of his wife and children with no particular emotion, the way a well-mannered widower makes it a point of honor not to let his grief distress his table companions, and finally, by not showing the slightest anxiety except over the sleeping pills they were giving him, which he worried might be habit-forming—a fear the psychiatrists found "displaced."

During subsequent interviews, although they saw him sob and show emphatic signs of misery, they couldn't say whether he was truly suffering or not. They had the uneasy sense of observing a robot deprived of all capacity to feel but programmed to analyze exterior stimuli and adapt its reactions accordingly. Used to functioning with the "Dr. Romand" program, he had needed an adjustment period to set up a new program, "Romand the murderer," and learn how to run it.

LUC RECEIVED A SHOCK TWO WEEKS AFTER THE FIRE WHEN he opened his mailbox and saw an envelope bearing the writing of this man more dead than alive. He opened it in terror, glanced at the contents, and sent the paper to the examining magistrate right away because he didn't want to keep it in his house. It was an insane letter in which the prisoner complained of the grotesque suspicions hanging over his head and asked Luc to find him a good lawyer. A few days earlier, Luc would have tried to believe that the truth lay in those wavering lines and not in the impressive collection of evidence amassed by the investigators. After first reporting Jean-Claude's denials, however, the newspapers had followed up with his confessions. By the time the letter arrived, it had lost all meaning.

When Luc came home from the burial service for Florence and the children, he sent Jean-Claude a note saying that the ceremony had been dignified and that the congregation had prayed for them and for him. He soon received another letter in which the prisoner alluded to having met "a chaplain who has greatly helped me to return to the Truth. But this reality is so horrible and difficult to bear that I'm afraid of hiding in a new imaginary world and losing a very shaky identity once more. The torment of having lost all my family and all my friends is so dreadful that I feel as though I were morally anesthetized. . . . Thank you for your prayers. They will help me to keep faith and bear up under this bereavement and this immense distress. I embrace you! I love you! . . . If you see any of Florence's friends or family, tell them I'm sorry."

Although he felt a rush of pity, Luc thought this piety was rather an easy refuge. On the other hand, who knows? His own faith forbade him to pass judgment. He did not answer the letter but showed it to one of Florence's brothers, Jean-Noël Crolet. The two men discussed it at length, agreeing that Jean-Claude talked a lot about his own ordeal and hardly at all about those he had "lost." As for the last sentence, it left Jean-Noël aghast: "What does he think? That remorse can be passed along like that? The way you'd say, Tell them hello from me?"

THE PSYCHIATRISTS SAW HIM AGAIN AT THE BEGINNING OF the summer. He was feeling chipper: he'd gotten back his glasses, which he had keenly missed in the first period of his incarceration, and a few personal effects. He volunteered the information that he had wanted to kill himself on May 1, the anniversary of his declaration of love to Florence, a date they had celebrated together every year. Determined not to botch it this time, he'd obtained what he needed to hang himself. But he'd dawdled a bit on the morning of the fateful day, long enough to learn on the radio that Pierre Bérégovoy, the former minister of finance, had just committed suicide. Disturbed at having let someone steal his thunder, seeing in this a sign that begged to be interpreted, he had put off carrying out his plan and then, after a meeting with the chaplain (an interview he calls decisive, though it was highly unlikely that a priest would have encouraged him to hang himself), he'd made a solemn resolution to abandon the idea. From that day on, he says, he "condemned himself to live" so as to dedicate his suffering to his family's memory. While remaining, according to the psychiatrists, extremely anxious to know what others thought of him, he began a period of prayer and meditation, accompanied by long fasts to prepare himself for the Eucharist. Thinner by fifty-five pounds, he feels he has left behind the labyrinth of false appearances to live in a world that is painful but "true." "The truth will set you free," said Christ. And Romand: "I have never been so free; life has never been so beautiful. I am a murderer, I'm seen as the lowest possible thing in society, but that's easier to bear than the twenty years of lies that came before." After some fumbling, the change of programs seems to have worked. The character of the respected researcher has been replaced by the no-less-gratifying character of the serious criminal on the road to mystical redemption.

Another team of psychiatrists took over from the first one and formulated the same diagnosis: the narcissistic narrative is continuing in prison, thus allowing its protagonist to avoid once again the massive depression with which he has been playing hide-and-seek all his life. At the same time, he is aware that every effort at comprehension on his part is viewed as a self-serving recovery and that the dice are loaded. "He will never, ever, manage to be perceived as authentic," the report concludes, "and he himself fears that he will never know if he is. Before, people believed everything he said; now no one believes anything anymore and he doesn't know what to believe, because he does not have access to his own truth but reconstructs it with the aid of the interpretations held out to him by the psychiatrists, the judge, the media. Insofar as he cannot be described at present as enduring great mental pain, it would seem difficult to impose on him a psychotherapeutic treatment he has not requested, contenting himself with making small talk with a volunteer prison visitor. One can only hope that, even at the risk of a melancholic depression (which remains a definite danger), he will become able to adjust to less rigid defenses and reach a level of more ambivalence and authenticity."

Leaving him, one of the psychiatrists said to his colleague, "If he weren't in prison, he'd be on the TV talk shows by now!"

THE LADMIRALS RECEIVED OTHER LETTERS, FOR EASTER, for the children's birthdays. The parents did not show them to their children. The letters made Luc extremely uneasy. He would read them quickly, then put them in the medical file of a fictitious patient, on the highest shelf in his office, where he went to get them for me. The last letter dates from the end of December.

". . . I let my thoughts and my prayers fly freely toward you, and they will reach you in the end, here or elsewhere. In spite of all that separates us, and your 'wounds that will never heal' (which I understand and which are legitimate), everything that brought us together in the past will perhaps reunite us beyond all time, in the communion of the living and the dead. May Christmas, which for us Christians is the symbol of the world saved by the Word made man, made child, be for you all a source of joy. I wish you a thousand blessings.

"P.S. Perhaps I was tactless in writing you for Sophie and Jérôme's birthdays. As I did today, I prayed before taking pen in hand, and these words have been dictated to me by a heartfelt impulse in communion with Florence, Caroline, and Antoine."

"Thank you for the thousand blessings you wish for us.

A few would do us nicely," Luc forced himself to write back, because it was Christmas. Their correspondence ended there.

That year and the two that followed were years of mourning and preparation for the trial. The Ladmirals lived like people who have almost perished in an earthquake and can no longer take a single step without apprehension. "Terra firma," one says—knowing that it's a trap. Nothing is firm or dependable anymore. It took them a long time to be able to trust anyone again. The children, like many of their classmates, were seen by a psychologist, the one who had called just after Florence's death to find out if she would be coming to evening Mass. Sophie felt guilty: if she had been there, her presence might have deterred her godfather. Cécile, however, thought he would have killed her, too, and thanked heaven her daughter hadn't spent that night, as she had so many others, at the Romands'. Cécile would burst into sobs whenever she found, slipped into books as page markers, old postcards from their friends. She couldn't stand dancing anymore, which she and Florence had loved so much. As for Luc, he was obsessed by the prospect of giving evidence. He was twice called before the examining magistrate in Bourg-en-Bresse. The judge seemed chilly to him at first, but he gradually warmed up, and Luc tried to make him understand that it was easy to see Romand as a monster and his friends as a bunch of ridiculously naive middle-class provincials when you knew how the story turned out, but that before then it was different. "It seems stupid to say this, but you know, he was a really nice guy. It doesn't change what he did at all, it makes it even more appalling, but he was *nice*." Despite the length of the interrogations, eight and ten hours, he came out of them racked by the anguish of having somehow missed the most important thing. He began to wake up at night to write down the memories coming back to him: a visit to Italy with Jean-Claude when they were eighteen; a conversation around a backyard barbecue; a dream that now seemed to him a premonition . . . His pre-occupation with composing a complete and coherent account he could give on the witness stand led him gradually to reread his whole life in the light of this friendship that had vanished into an abyss, almost taking along with it everything he believed in.

His testimony was misconstrued, and this wounded him. In the press section, some even pitied the accused for having had for a best friend this smug, straitlaced guy. I later realized that he had crammed as though for an oral exam and that this exam was the most important one of his life. It had to justify his life. No wonder he was tense.

It's over now. The man I went to see after the trial feels that he and his family have "passed through the flames and come out safely on the other side." Traces remain, their footsteps are sometimes shaky, but they're back on solid ground. While we were talking, Sophie came home from school and without lowering his voice he continued in her presence to speak of the man who had been her godfather. She was twelve years old; she listened to us gravely and attentively. She even piped up to add further details, and I thought it was a huge victory for this family finally to be able to speak so freely about what had hurt them so deeply.

Luc, on certain days of grace, is able to pray for the prisoner but neither to write nor to visit him. It's a question of survival. He thinks Jean-Claude has "chosen hell on earth." As a Christian, he is profoundly troubled by this, but Christianity, he says, makes room for mystery. He submits. He accepts not understanding everything.

He has just been elected president of the school board of Saint-Vincent.

The gray plastic bags still haunt his dreams.

The woman who ran toward the prisoner calling his name when he collapsed for the second time, as he was recounting the deaths of his children, was Marie-France. She is a prison visitor and began seeing him in Lyon, shortly after he emerged from his coma. She continued to visit him each week in Bourg-en-Bresse. It was she who gave him *Class Trip*. At first glance, she seems like an unassuming little lady in her late fifties dressed in navy blue. A second look reveals something striking about her, a lively yet serene quality she has that puts people immediately at their ease. My plan to write Jean-Claude's story inspired in her a confidence that I found surprising and that I wasn't certain I deserved.

All through the account of the murders, she couldn't stop thinking of the terrible time he'd had earlier, during the reconstructions of the crimes back in December 1994. She'd been afraid he wouldn't survive them. In Prévessin, he had at first refused to leave the police van. Finally he had gone inside the house and even upstairs. Entering his bedroom, he thought something supernatural would happen—perhaps that he'd be struck by lightning. He proved unable to go through the motions corresponding to his descriptions. A policeman lay down on the bed and another officer, armed with a rolling pin, pretended to strike him in different postures. Jean-Claude had to give orders, correct mistakes, like a movie director. I'd seen the photos of these reconstructions: they were sinister and at the same time somewhat farcical. Next, they moved to the children's bedroom, where they'd placed on what remained of the beds two little mannequins dressed in pajamas purchased for the occasion (the bills for which appear in the dossier). The examining magistrate wanted him to pick up the rifle but he couldn't: he fainted. He spent the rest of the day downstairs, sitting in an armchair, while a policeman played his role. The second floor had been ravaged by the fire, but the living room was exactly as it had been on his return from Paris Sunday morning, including the children's drawings and the crowns from the Twelfth Night cake. The magistrate had the cassettes from the VCR and the answering machine placed under seal; several days later, he had Jean-Claude listen to the incoming-message tape. That's when lightning did strike. The first message still on the tape was from the previous summer. It was the voice of Florence, quite gay, quite affectionate, saying, "Hi there, it's us, we arrived safely, we're waiting for you to join us, be careful on the road, we love you." And Antoine, after her: "I'm sending you a big kiss, Papa, I love you, I love you, I love you, come quickly." The magistrate, hearing that and watching him listen to it, began to weep. After that, Jean-Claude could not stop hearing that message. He kept repeating those words that broke his heart and at the same time consoled him. They arrived safely. They're waiting for me. They love me. I have to be careful on the road that leads me to them.

SINCE SHE HAD OBTAINED PERMISSION TO SEE HIM BETWEEN court sessions, I asked Marie-France if she knew about the story I'd heard from his lawyer, how on the first day of the trial he remembered—in a sort of blinding flash—the real reason for his initial evasion so many years ago.

"Oh, yes! Abad didn't want him to mention it because it wasn't in the file, and according to him it would have upset the jury. I think he was wrong, it was important for them to know it. The morning of the final exam, as he was leaving to go take it, Jean-Claude found a letter in his mailbox. It was from a young woman who was in love with him and whom he had rejected because he loved Florence. The young woman wrote him that when he opened that letter she would be dead. She had killed herself. That's why—it's because he felt so guilty over her death that he didn't go take the exam. That's how it all started."

I was dumbfounded.

"Wait a minute. You believe this story?"

Marie-France looked at me in astonishment.

"Why would he lie?"

"I don't know. Actually, yes, I do know. Because he lies. That's his mode of being, he can't do otherwise, and I think he does it more to fool himself than to fool others. If this story is true, someone should be able to verify it. Maybe not verify that a girl he knew committed suicide over him but at least that a girl he knew committed suicide at that time. All he has to do is give her name."

"He doesn't want to. Out of respect for her family."

"Naturally. He doesn't want to say who the researcher was from whom he bought the cancer-medicine capsules, either. Well, unlike you, I think Abad was more than right to tell him to keep that story to himself."

My disbelief worried Marie-France. She herself was so incapable of lying that the idea of his making up this cock-eyed tale had never crossed her mind.

ABAD HAD SUMMONED HER AS A WITNESS FOR THE DEFENSE and was counting on her to correct the impression the preceding witness was sure to make for the prosecution. He'd give anything, he confided to me with a gloomy sigh, not to be around when that witness took the stand.

Mme. Milo, a petite blonde no longer in the first flush of youth but stylish and attractive, was the teacher whose affair with the principal had caused a scandal at the Ecole Saint-Vincent. She began by alluding to the "difficult moments" the two of them had lived through and the support given them by the Romands. A few months after the tragedy, the former principal had received from the prison in Bourg-en-Bresse a letter that was a cry for help. He had showed it to her, and she had been touched. They separated when he then left to run a school in the Midi. Mme. Milo began to write to the prisoner. She had been Antoine's teacher; the little boy's death had utterly traumatized the pupils in her nursery school class: they talked about it constantly, and her teaching was turning into group therapy. One day she asked the children to make a lovely drawing together "to give courage to someone in trouble," and without telling them that the person in trouble was the father and murderer of Antoine, she sent the drawing to him from all of them. He replied with an effusive letter, which she read in class.

Abad bent abruptly over his papers, while the prosecutor nodded pensively. Mme. Milo, sensing the uneasiness, fell silent. The judge had to intervene.

"You visited Jean-Claude Romand in prison and began an amorous relationship with him."

"I wouldn't say that . . ."

"The guards observed 'voluptuous embraces' in the visiting room."

"I wouldn't say that . . ."

"In the correspondence impounded by the court Jean-Claude Romand addressed this poem to you:

> "I wanted to write you
> a *je ne sais quoi*,
> something sweet, something serene,
> from the realm of the unseen,
> a *je ne sais quoi*,
> something pleasant
> something pleasing
> a *je ne sais quoi*
> that calms
> that charms
> a *je ne sais quoi*
> that gives confidence
> even in silence
> so I'm here to tell you
> an 'I love you' "

In the shocked silence that followed this reading (I've rarely experienced a more *uncomfortable* moment and I feel that same discomfort again as I transcribe my notes today), the witness mumbled that she'd put all that behind her, she now had another companion and no longer saw Jean-Claude Romand.

We thought the ordeal was over, but he had, besides this poem, sent a letter containing excerpts from Camus's novel *The Fall*, which he said expressed his thoughts very well. The prosecutor began to read.

"If I'd been able to kill myself and afterward see their faces, then yes, it would have been worth it. People aren't convinced of your sincerity, your motives, and the depth of your sorrows except by your death. As long as you are alive, your case is uncertain, and you are entitled only to their skepticism. So if one were sure to enjoy the spectacle, it would be worth it to prove to them what they don't wish to believe, and to astonish them. But you kill yourself and what does it matter whether they believe you or not: you aren't there to drink in their amazement and their contrition (so fleeting, moreover), to attend, as every man dreams, your own funeral."

Romand had copied out eight long pages in this vein, which the prosecutor reveled in reading, ending his selections with what he described as a profession of faith: "Above all do not believe your friends when they ask you to be sincere with them. If you should find yourself in this situation, do not hesitate: promise to be truthful and lie as best you can."

The accused tried to explain himself.

"All that describes my life from before . . . I know now that it's the opposite, that only the truth sets you free."

The effect, as Abad had foreseen, was devastating. Coming immediately afterward, Marie-France, poor thing, never had a chance. She began by movingly recalling her first meetings with the prisoner. "When I'd shake his hand, I felt as though I were shaking hands with a dead man, he was so cold. He thought only of dying—I never saw anyone so sad. . . . Every time I said good-bye, I thought I wouldn't see him the next visiting hour. And then one day, in May of 1993, he told me, 'Marie-France, I condemn myself to life. I have decided to assume that suffering for Florence's family, for my friends.' And after that, everything changed." And after that, too, her testimony stopped being convincing. Everyone thought about the little poem, about that absurd idyll with Antoine's former teacher, and this made her pious words ridiculous when she spoke of "the forgiveness he cannot expect from others because he does not forgive himself." Not realizing this, she wound up by presenting Jean-Claude as a wonderful fellow to whom the other prisoners came to gather new strength, *joie de vivre*, and optimism: a ray of sunshine. While the prosecutor listened to this defense witness with the smile of a well-fed cat, Abad literally shrank into his barrister's robe.

IT WAS THE SECOND-TO-LAST EVENING OF THE TRIAL; ONLY the summations to the court remained. I had dinner with a group of journalists, among them a veteran reporter named

Martine Servandoni, who had been outraged by Marie-France's testimony. She found her sweetness-and-light act not only laughable but irresponsible, and frankly criminal. Romand, she went on, was a creep, and of the worst kind, flabby and sentimental like his poem. That said, since the death penalty had been abolished, he was going to live, to spend twenty or thirty years in prison, and we were thus clearly obliged to consider the question of his psychological and spiritual future. From this point of view, the only positive thing that could happen would be for him to *truly* realize what he had done and, instead of sniveling, to *truly* sink into the severe depression he'd spent his whole life scrambling to avoid. Only at such a cost was there a chance he might one day accede to something that was not a lie, not another flight from reality. Which meant that the worst thing that could happen to him was for church hens like Marie-France to bring him a new role on a silver platter, the part of the great sinner who expiates his crime by saying the rosary. For that kind of moron, Martine would not have opposed the reinstatement of the death penalty. And she didn't mind telling me that she considered Marie-France and me two of a kind. "He must be just thrilled that you're writing a book on him! That's what he's dreamed about his whole life. So it was a good thing that he killed his parents—all his wishes have come true. People talk about him, he's on TV, someone's writing his biography, and he's well on his way to becoming a saint. That's what you call coming out on top. Brilliant performance. I say, Bravo!"

"PEOPLE WILL SPEAK TO YOU OF COMPASSION. I RESERVE mine for the victims"—that's how the prosecutor began his summation to the jury, which lasted four hours. The accused was portrayed as a Machiavellian pervert who "took up duplicity the way one takes holy orders," enjoying every moment of his imposture. In this trial where the facts themselves were not in doubt, the sincerity of Romand's desire to commit suicide turned out to be the main stake in the duel between the prosecution and the defense. After rereading, in a toneless voice, the excruciating account of the children's murder, the prosecutor burst out dramatically: "Enough! This is madness! After that, what possible reaction could a father have, except to turn his weapon on himself? But no, he puts it away, goes out for the newspapers, the vendor finds him calm and courteous, and even today he remembers that he didn't buy *L'Equipe*! Once his parents have been killed in their turn, he's still in no hurry to join them in the other world. He continues to wait, to give himself reprieves, perhaps hoping for one of those famous miracles that have always rescued him until now. After leaving Corinne, he goes home and lets some twenty hours go by, hoping for what? That she will file a complaint? That someone will discover the bodies at Clairvaux? That the police will come for him before the fatal deed? He finally decides to set the fire, but at four in the morning, the precise time the street cleaners go by. He starts it in the attic, so that the flames can be seen quickly and from a long way off. He waits for the firemen to arrive before he swallows a handful of pills ten years beyond their expiration date. And to top it off, in case they take their time, thinking the house is empty, he indicates his presence by opening the window. The psychiatrists talk about 'ordalian' behavior, meaning that he placed himself in the hands of fate. Fine. Death didn't want him. Coming out of his coma, does he choose on his own that path of painful expiation described by noble souls? Not at all. He denies, he invents the story of the mysterious man in black who killed his family before his very eyes."

Carried away by his performance, making much of the fact that a collection of crime mysteries on the theme of the locked room was found at the foot of Romand's bed, the prosecutor went so far as to imagine a diabolical plan, lucidly carried out, not only to survive but even to be declared innocent. Abad had no trouble pointing out that this diabolical plan would have been ridiculously inept. In his plea for the defense, a speech as vehement as his opponent's had been scathing, he argued that Romand, already accused of multiple murder and fraudulent misuse of funds, should not be blamed as well for not having killed himself. But clearly, emotionally speaking, that's exactly what he was being blamed for.

• • •

THE LAST WORDS IN A FRENCH TRIAL, BEFORE THE COURT
retires to deliberate, belong to the accused. Romand had
obviously prepared his text and he read it without any mistakes, in a voice that sometimes broke with emotion:

"It's true that silence must be my lot. I understand that
my words and even my still being alive make the scandal of
my actions worse. I wished to take upon myself both judgment and punishment and I believe that this is the last time
I will be able to speak to those who suffer because of me. I
know that my words are pathetically inadequate, but I must
speak. I must tell them their anguish is with me day and
night. I know they refuse to forgive me, but in memory of
Florence I want to ask their forgiveness. It will perhaps come
to me only after my death. I want to tell Florence's mother
and brothers that her father died as a result of his fall. I don't
ask them to believe me, because I have no proof, but I say
it before Florence and before God because I know that an
unconfessed crime will not be forgiven. I ask them all to
forgive me.

"Now it is to you, my Flo, to you, my Caro, my Titou,
my Papa, my Mama, that I would like to speak. You are
here in my heart and it is this invisible presence that gives
me the strength to speak to you. You know everything, and
if anyone can forgive me, it is you. I ask your forgiveness.
Forgiveness for having destroyed your lives, forgiveness for
having never told the truth. And yet, my Flo, I am sure that

with your intelligence, your goodness, your mercy, you could have found it in your heart to pardon me. Forgive me for not having been able to bear the thought of causing you pain. I knew that I couldn't live without you, but I am still alive today and I promise you I will try to live as long as God wishes me to, unless those who suffer because of me ask me to die to relieve their torment. I know that you will help me to find the path of truth, of life. There was a great, great deal of love between us. I will still love you in truth. I ask forgiveness of those who can forgive. I ask forgiveness as well of those who can never forgive.

"Thank you, Your Honor."

AFTER FIVE HOURS OF DELIBERATION, JEAN-CLAUDE Romand was condemned to life imprisonment, with no possibility of parole for twenty-two years. If all goes well, he will be released in 2015, when he is sixty-one.

Paris, November 21, 1996

Dear Jean-Claude Romand,

It has been three months now since I began writing. My problem is not, as I thought it would be in the beginning, gathering information. It's finding my proper place with respect to your story. When I began work, I thought I could push this problem aside by stitching together everything I knew and trying to remain objective. But objectivity, in such an undertaking, is a delusion. I needed a point of view. I went to see your friend Luc and asked him to tell me how he and his family lived through the days following the discovery of the crime. That is what I tried to write, identifying myself with him all the more because he had told me he did not want to appear in my book under his real name, but I soon judged it impossible (technically and morally—the two go together) to maintain this point of view. That's why the half-joking suggestion you made in your last letter, of adopting the viewpoint of your successive dogs, both amused me and convinced me that you were aware of this difficulty. A difficulty that is obviously much greater for you than for me and that is at stake in the psychological and spiritual work in which you are engaged: this lack of access to yourself, this void that has never stopped growing in place of the person in you who must say "I." Clearly, I am not the one who will say "I" on your behalf, but in writing about you, I still need to say—in my own name and without hiding behind a more or less imaginary witness or a patchwork of information intended to be objective—what speaks to me in your life and resonates in mine. Well, I cannot. Words slip away from me; the "I" sounds false. So I've decided to set this project aside, as it is not yet ripe. But I would not like this hiatus to bring our correspondence to an end. Actually, I feel it will be easier to write, and doubtless to listen, to you once I have set aside this project in which we each had an immediate interest. Without it, we should be able to speak more freely . . .

Villefranche-sur-Saône, 12/10/96

Dear Emmanuel Carrère,

I well understand your situation. I appreciate the sincerity and courage of your attitude, which makes you accept the disappointment of failure after considerable work on a project rather than be satisfied with an account that would not meet your objective.

What still gives me a little strength today is, first of all, not being alone in this search for the truth, and I feel as well that I'm beginning to perceive that meaningful inner voice that until now has been unable to manifest itself except through symptoms or acting out. I feel intuitively that I must find within myself a voice that is confirmed by listening attentively to what truly speaks in another person. It also seems to me that this impossibility of saying "I" when you speak of me is partly related to my own difficulty in saying "I" for myself. Even if I manage to reach this stage, it will be too late, and it is cruel to think that if I had had access to this "I" and therefore to "you" and "we" at the appropriate time, I would have been able to tell them everything I had to say to them without violence making the rest of the dialogue impossible. In spite of everything, to despair would be to give up once again and, like you, I believe that time will permit a transformation, will bring some sense to all this. Writing these words, I think of something Claudel wrote: "Time is the sense of life," as one would speak of the sense of a word, the sense of smell, or the direction in which a river flows. . . . When time makes sense out of this terrible reality, reality will become the truth and will perhaps be something quite different from the one that seemed obvious. If it really is the truth, it will contain its own remedy for everyone concerned. . . ."

As I had predicted to him (without entirely believing it), our correspondence became easier once I abandoned the book. He began to talk about the present, his life in prison. From Bourg-en-Bresse, he had been transferred to the detention facility in Villefranche-sur-Saône. Marie-France went there to see him every week, along with another visitor, named Bernard. At first Romand feared the brutal assaults customarily inflicted on child murderers, but a gang leader soon recognized him and assured him of his protection. One day, back when they were both on the outside, Romand had picked him up hitchhiking and had given him a two-hundred-franc bill so he could buy himself a good meal. This generosity had erased the horror of his crimes and made him popular. The prize celebrity of Villefranche, Alain Carignon, a former mayor of Grenoble in jail for corruption, invited Romand to go jogging with him. Whenever a difficult prisoner arrived, the authorities placed him in Romand's cell, counting on his calming influence. He took care of the library, attended computer classes, participated in comic-strip and writing workshops. Eager to become absorbed in some long-term project, he began to study Japanese. And when I spoke to him about the long-term project I myself was embarking on, a new translation of the Bible, a collaboration among scholars and writers, he was immediately enthusiastic. Since I was assigned the Gospel According to Saint Mark, he read that with particular devotion, comparing the five translations available to him in the library, and took pleasure in informing me that Marie-France's great-uncle was none other than Father Lagrange, who had over-seen the translation of the Jerusalem Bible. There was discussion of my coming to Villefranche to lead a workshop on my project sponsored by the chaplain, but Romand was transferred before the plan could be realized.

I went to see him only once. That visit, which I had dreaded, went well, almost too well. I was relieved and a little shocked. What was I expecting? That having done what he had done and survived it, he would go around in sackcloth and ashes, beating his breast, rolling on the ground every five minutes wailing in agony? He had gained back some weight since the trial, and aside from the sloppy uniform that is standard prison garb, he looked as he must have when he was the affable Dr. Romand. Obviously happy to see me, he did the honors and showed me around the visiting room, apologizing for its lack of comforts. He smiled a bit too much, as did I. There were no lengthy silences or Dostoyevskian effusions. We spoke of this and that, like people who have met on vacation (in our case, it had been in the criminal court in Bourg-en-Bresse) and, without knowing one another well, have discovered some mutual interests. Not a word about the past.

In his next letter, he asked me the name of my cologne.

"This probably seems absurd to you, but I think I know the scent, and maybe by identifying it I will recover the memories attached to it. You are perhaps aware that Florence had a passion for perfume; she prized her collection of samples, several hundred little bottles she'd been acquiring since adolescence. I had occasion to experience, during the reconstruction of the tragedy, the close links between the nerve centers of olfaction and memory when I recognized a familiar perfume. . . ."

I was touched by the unaffected, friendly aspect of his request, but even more by this: in the almost three years that we had been corresponding, it was the first time that—instead of talking about "my family," "those who loved me," or "my dear ones"—he had written his wife's first name.

When I told him, two years later, that I was getting back to work, he was not surprised. He had expected it, although perhaps not so soon. And he was confident.

Marie-France also thought this was good news. I called to collect the dossier. According to law, the convicted person remains the owner of the original file, but since it takes up quite a bit of space, and the cells are small, and the lockers at the entrances to prisons are overloaded, Romand had deposited his dossier with Marie-France. Her advice, when she invited me to come get it, was to clean out my car trunk thoroughly if I wanted to fit in all the boxes. I gathered that she was not displeased to be passing this sinister business on to me and that by bringing it back to Paris I was committing myself to keeping it until he got out.

She lives in a village thirty miles east of Lyon. I'd had no sense of her background and was surprised to find an immense and magnificent house surrounded by a park that sloped gently down toward the Ain River. The spot is delightful, and the house is opulently furnished. Marie-France had told me to come during the week, when it's quiet, because she and her husband have a number of children and grandchildren who come for the weekend, rarely fewer than twenty of them. Raph, the husband, was a textile manufacturer before he retired. Marie-France herself comes from a line of Lyonese silk merchants, and until her children were all grown, she led the life of a mother and housewife, slightly more devout as a Christian than most. If you press her to tell you, she will say that when she reached fifty she heard a call. She was to go to prison. To prison? It took her some time to understand and allow herself to be persuaded, as she is not a religious fanatic. Besides, you don't become a prison visitor overnight. There is a probation period during which you welcome and give support to the families of prisoners before and after visiting hours. I'd been struck at Villefranche by the atmosphere created by these kind souls in the mobile home at the prison gate that serves as a waiting room. Thanks to them, it's not too grim; they offer coffee, people talk to one another, and those coming for the first time don't have to learn the rules the hard way. After this apprenticeship, Marie-France crossed the threshold and has since assisted with her friendship dozens of prisoners in the

Lyon area. Jean-Claude, whom she has known for almost six years now, is clearly one of her favorites. She knows all about his torments and his mental fragility (it wouldn't take very much, in her opinion, for him to relapse into despair and kill himself), but she admires as a gift from God his ability to look "on the bright side of life," in spite of everything. "And then it's easy to help him, you see. It does you good when someone is easy to help. When I see him, he often repeats to me something I told him the last time I visited and he assures me that it has helped him get through the week. This cheers me up."

This goodwill, which makes him a gratifying client for a prison visitor, has won him another guardian angel, Bernard, whom he had mentioned in his letters to me. Marie-France had invited Bernard and his wife to lunch with us. The day before, Bernard had made the trip from Lyon to Paris and back to go see Jean-Claude in Fresnes, where he had just been transferred. Rudely torn from surroundings that had become familiar, Jean-Claude had found himself in a strange place, among strangers, treated like a package in a sorting room, and Bernard, who is seventy-five years old, had thought it only natural to set right off on the train so that the new inmate might see a friendly face for at least a half hour. I who had gone only once to Villefranche felt vaguely ashamed, especially since Bernard must have had to force himself to go through the gate at Fresnes, a place that brings back painful memories for him. Condemned to death as a member of the

Resistance, he was imprisoned there by the Gestapo and lived for two months in the expectation of execution. His only reading material was a copy of the writings of Saint Thérèse de Lisieux, thanks to whom he was converted and ceased to fear death. In the end, he was deported. He spent four days en route to Buchenwald in a locked boxcar without food or anything to drink but urine, huddled among the dying, most of whom were corpses by the time the journey was over. I would never claim that such an experience necessarily endows a man with infallible lucidity later on, but I mention it to make clear that Bernard is not a sacristan who knows nothing of evil and life. And when this rather right-wing, rather conservative elderly Gaullist speaks of the crook and murderer Jean-Claude Romand as a charming fellow whom he is always pleased to see, one can tell that he does so not from any charitable obligation but from real friendship.

After lunch, we went out onto the terrace overlooking the Ain and the surrounding open country, which seemed to me remarkably hilly for a plain. It was Indian summer; the trees were a russet color, the sky was very blue, and thrushes were singing. We enjoyed sunshine and coffee while eating Swiss chocolates. Raph, who looks a bit like the French actor Philippe Noiret, listened benevolently to his wife and his friend Bernard speaking about their protégé. By this time, Raph felt as though he knew him. And he liked him. "So," he said to me, "are you a member of the club, too?" I didn't know how to answer. I didn't want to abuse the trust of these people by making them believe that I was, like them, unconditionally devoted to Jean-Claude. To me, he was not "Jean-Claude." I had begun my letters to him at first with "Monsieur," then "Dear Monsieur," then "Dear Jean-Claude Romand," but I would have stuck at "Dear Jean-Claude." Listening to Marie-France and Bernard animatedly discussing his winter wardrobe ("He already has the blue pullover, which is warm, but it would be good if he also had the gray Polarfleece sweater; perhaps Emmanuel could take it to him . . ."), I found their affection—so straightforward, so natural—both admirable and almost monstrous. Not only was I myself not capable of it, but I did not wish to be. I did not wish to take the path that would allow me to swallow unflinchingly a fabrication as blatant as the story of the rejected lover who killed herself on the day before the exam, or to believe like Bernard that at bottom this tragic fate was providential: "To think that it should have taken all those lies, those random accidents, and that terrible tragedy so that today he might do all the good he does around him. It's something I've always believed, you see, and that I see at work in Jean-Claude's life: everything works out and finds its meaning in the end for those who love God."

I was just speechless. But no doubt so were the people who listened in 1887 to little Thérèse Martin, not yet de Lisieux, pray to God to pardon Henri Pranzini, the brutal murderer of two women and a little girl. I was perfectly aware that Bernard's attitude, which I found so scandalous, was simply that of a deeply committed Christian. I wound up imagining Marie-France and Bernard leaning over my work to one side of me, rejoicing even more—and all heaven with them—for a repentant sinner than for the ninety-nine just souls who have no need to repent; on my other side, I heard Martine Servandoni saying that the worst thing that could happen to Romand would be to fall into the hands of those people, let himself be lulled by angelic speeches on the infinite mercy of the Lord and the wonders He would work in his soul, and thus lose all chance of someday getting back in touch with reality. One could obviously maintain that in a case like his, that might be preferable, but Martine felt that in every case, without exception, painful lucidity was better than soothing illusion, and I'm not one to argue with her about that.

BERNARD AND HIS WIFE BELONG TO A CATHOLIC MOVE-ment called the Intercessors, who organize shifts to ensure a chain of uninterrupted prayer. At any given moment in France, and I believe throughout the world, there is at least one intercessor praying. Each one signs up for a certain time and date, and Jean-Claude, recruited by Bernard, has been zealous in choosing unpopular time slots, for example from two to four in the morning. Bernard asked him to bear witness about his experience and published his statement anonymously in the group's newsletter:

"Since I have been in prison for several years, condemned to a life sentence after a terrible family tragedy, naturally you would not think my situation would lead me to bear witness, but speaking as one intercessor among two thousand others about the Grace and Love of God, I will try to give thanks to Him.

"The ordeal of incarceration but above all the trials of mourning and despair should have separated me forever from God. Encounters with a chaplain and two prison visitors blessed with the gift of listening and of speaking frankly, without judging, have released me from the exile of unspeakable suffering that cut me off from God and the rest of humanity. Today, I know that these providential helping hands were for me the first manifestations of divine Grace.

"Events of a mystical nature, not easy to communicate, have deeply stirred me and become the foundations of my new faith. Among the most striking: during a night of insomnia and anguish, when I felt more than ever guilty for living, the presence of God burst upon me unexpectedly as I contemplated in the darkness the Holy Face painted by Rouault. After the most dreadful despondency, my tears were no longer those of sadness but the result of an inner fire and of the profound Peace that comes from the certainty of being loved.

"Prayer has an essential place in my life. It is harder than one would imagine to fall silent and pray in a cell. Finding the time certainly isn't a problem; the main obstacle is the noise of radios, TVs, and shouting from windows that lasts late into the night. Often, saying prayers for a while, mechanically, without paying attention to the meaning of the words, allows one to neutralize the surrounding din and the static of thought before finding the peace conducive to a personal prayer.

"When I was free, I had heard, without paying much attention or feeling in any way concerned, these words from the Gospel: 'I was in prison and you visited me' (Matthew 25:36). I had the good fortune to become acquainted with the Intercessors thanks to one of these visitors, now a most dear friend. These two hours of prayer every month, at a very late hour when the difference between the outside world and the inner world fades away, are blessed moments. The struggle against sleep that precedes them is always rewarded. It is a joy to be able to be a link in this continuous chain of prayer that banishes isolation and the feeling of uselessness. It is also reassuring for me to feel, in the depths of the abyss that is prison, that there remain these invisible safety ropes to keep us from going under: prayers. I often think of this image of the rope one must cling to so that I may remain faithful, at all costs, to the appointment of these hours of intercession.

"In discovering that Grace is not in the fulfillment of my desires, even though they may be generous and altruistic, but in the strength to accept everything with joy, from the depths of my cell my *De Profundis* becomes *Magnificat* and all is Light."

DRIVING BACK TO PARIS TO SET TO WORK, I NO LONGER saw any mystery in his long imposture, only a pathetic mixture of blindness, cowardice, and distress. What went on in his head during those empty hours dragged out in highway rest stops or parking lots was something I was familiar with, having experienced it in my own way, and it was no longer any of my business. But what goes on in his heart now, in the hours of the night when he stays awake to pray?

I unloaded the trunk, and as I put the boxes of files away for the next twenty years in a closet in my studio, I understood that I would never open them again. The account written at Bernard's request, however, lay open on my table. I found its wooden Catholic jargon truly mysterious. In the logical sense, *undecidable*.

He is not putting on an act, of that I'm sure, but isn't the liar inside him putting one over on him? When Christ enters his heart, when the certainty of being loved in spite of everything makes tears of joy run down his cheeks, isn't it the adversary deceiving him yet again?

I thought that writing this story could only be either a crime or a prayer.

Paris, January 1999

ABOUT THE AUTHOR

Emmanuel Carrère, one of France's most critically acclaimed writers, is the author of screenplays, a forthcoming biography of Philip K. Dick, and five novels, including *The Mustache* and *Class Trip*, which won the prestigious Prix Femina. A major bestseller in France, *The Adversary* is being published in eighteen countries. Carrère lives in Paris.